ADVANCED HARMONY

Theory and Practice

Second Edition

ROBERT W. OTTMAN

Professor of Music
North Texas State University
Denton, Texas

PRENTICE-HALL, INC., Englewood Cliffs, New Jersey

Printed in the United States of America

ISBN: 0-13-012955-0

Library of Congress Catalog Card No.: 72-173655

10 9 8 7 6 5 4 3

PRENTICE-HALL INTERNATIONAL, INC., London
PRENTICE-HALL OF AUSTRALIA, PTY. LTD., Sydney
PRENTICE-HALL OF CANADA, LTD., Toronto
PRENTICE-HALL OF INDIA PRIVATE LTD., New Delhi
PRENTICE-HALL OF JAPAN, INC., Tokyo

Contents

Preface

Elementary Harmony: Theory and Practice and its companion volume, *Advanced Harmony: Theory and Practice,* are designed to meet the needs of college courses in basic music theory, including instruction in the four related areas: written harmony, keyboard harmony, ear training, and sight singing. The subject matter of each chapter and its application to each of these four areas are so presented that they can be taught successfully either in the correlated class (all four areas in one class) or in several classes, each devoted to one or more of these areas.

The texts are based on the techniques of composers of the seventeenth to nineteenth centuries. They include a comprehensive survey of the harmonic materials used in these historical periods, from the simple triad through seventh chords, altered chords, ninth, eleventh, and thirteenth chords, and simple and complex methods of modulation. The historical limitation in no way implies that teaching of music theory must be limited to this period. But for the undergraduate student, knowledge of the practices of the seventeenth and nineteenth centuries should serve as a point of departure for his study of both pre-seventeenth-century music and twentieth-century music.

In addition to the theoretical presentation, a comprehensive practical application of these harmonic materials is presented. Concurrent studies in melodic and rhythmic analysis and composition, in harmonic analysis, in instrumentation, and in analysis of form (small forms only) implement this application. With these materials, the student is not only asked to solve traditional figured bass exercises, but is led ultimately to accomplishments in arranging given melodies and in creating original music, in both vocal and instrumental styles. *Advanced Harmony* presents a comprehensive study of instrumental styles of writing, based on the principles of four-voice writing learned in the previous volume. This study is applied to the realization of Baroque figured basses for solo instrument or voice with keyboard accompaniment, to the harmonization of melodic lines in instrumental style, to setting texts for vocal solo and accompaniment, and to the composition of music for solo piano or solo orchestral instrument with keyboard accompaniment.

Continuing the policy begun in *Elementary Harmony* of placing these theoretical studies in historical context, Chapter 14 of *Advanced Harmony* offers a preview of the principal compositional techniques of the twentieth century, and the relationship of these to techniques of the eighteenth and nineteenth centuries as covered in previous chapters.

There are several other features that will be of particular interest:

Part-Writing. The principles of part-writing are codified, making possible easy reference to any part-writing procedure. (See Appendix 1.)

Musical Examples. Hundreds of examples covering a wide range of composers, nationalities, and periods are presented. Examples early in the course are principally in four-part vocal structure. As the text advances, more of the examples are in instrumental style.

Terminology. Unfortunately, there is no standard terminology in music theory. Students often complete a theory course or even attain a degree in music but are unable to understand many articles in the literature of music theory or musicology. This text lists and describes at appropriate places the more important of these varying terminologies.

The method of identification of chords by roman numeral symbols is explained in Chapter 2 of *Elementary Harmony* and at appropriate places in later chapters. Teaching procedures and materials, especially in keyboard harmony and ear training, require chord symbols which, when stated alone and without reference to staff notation, will spell the given chord (diatonic or altered) when the key is known. Chosen for this purpose are the "quality" symbols, where the quality of the sound is reflected in the symbol (I = major, i = minor, etc.), combined with the "functional" symbols for certain altered harmonies (V of V, etc.).

Self-Help in Ear Training. Most chapters contain projects in self-help in ear training, enabling the student to work on this vital aspect of his theoretical training outside of class.

Assignments and Exercises. Material for student participation is divided into "Assignments"—that which can be committed to paper—and "Exercises" —that which can be demonstrated only by speaking or singing or at the keyboard.

Supplementary Materials. Assignments in sight singing and in melodic analysis and melody harmonization are made from the author's *Music for Sight Singing.* Many references besides those illustrated are made to the collection of 371 Chorales by Johann Sebastian Bach; also, a number of assignments in harmonic and melodic analysis are made from this collection.

In appropriate places throughout both volumes, assignments in harmonic analysis are made from these five additional collections of music: Beethoven, Sonatas for Piano (numbers 1–12 only); Chopin, Mazurkas; Mendelssohn, *Songs Without Words;* Mozart, Sonatas for Piano; and Schumann, *Album for the Young,* Op. 68. Many students will already own some or all of these.

All the procedures and materials in these texts have been tested for many years through use in the music theory courses at North Texas State University. The author acknowledges his indebtedness to the many hundreds of undergraduate and graduate students whose participation in the presentation and study of these materials has made the final form of the text possible. Particular thanks are due the members of the NTSU theory faculty, Frank Mainous, Alan Richardson, and William Gardner, for their cooperation in teaching these materials on an experimental basis and for their many able suggestions and constructive criticisms resulting from this classroom experience.

Robert W. Ottman

1

Modulation to Closely Related Keys

THEORY AND ANALYSIS[1]

A change of key occurs during the course of many musical compositions. The piece will begin in accordance with the key signature, progress to one or more different keys, often without change of key signature, and return to the original key before the closing measures. The study of modulation includes the relationship of keys used in a composition and the methods of progression from one key to another.

Relationship of Keys

In a modulation, a key may progress to any other key. The keys to which it may progress are divided into two groups:

1. *Closely related keys.* There are five keys closely related to any given key. These can be identified in several ways, three of which are as follows:

   a) The closely related key has a signature the same as, or one accidental more or less than, the original key. The closely related keys to D major (two sharps) consist of all the keys with a signature of one sharp, two sharps, or three sharps—G major, E minor, B minor, A major, and F♯ minor.

---

[1]This chapter follows the elementary study of modulation as presented in Chapter 20 of the author's *Elementary Harmony: Theory and Practice,* 2nd ed. (Englewood Cliffs, N.J.: Prentice-Hall, Inc., 1970). Included in Chapter 20 are (1) modulation from a major key to its dominant, (2) modulation from a minor key to its relative major, (3) the transient modulation, and (4) the supertonic major triad (II or VofV) in major and minor keys.

b) A closely related key is one whose tonic triad is found as a diatonic major or minor triad in the original key. In D major, the diatonic triads are ii, E minor; iii, F♯ minor; IV, G major; V, A major; and vi, B minor.

In a minor key, calculation of the diatonic triads is made on the basis of the natural (pure) minor scale. In D minor the closely related keys are III, F major; iv, G minor; v, A minor; VI, B♭ major; and VII, C major.

c) The tonic, dominant, and subdominant keys and their related keys produce the six closely related keys.

D major:		D		B	
	G		A	E	F♯
	(major	keys)		(minor	keys)
D minor:		D		F	
	G		A	B♭	C
	(minor	keys)		(major	keys)

Modulation may be made from keys with seven accidentals to keys with eight accidentals, though no key signatures exist for the latter and such modulations are quite uncommon. For examples, see Bach, *Well-tempered Clavier*, Volume 2, Prelude No. 3, measures 1–6 for a modulation from C♯ major to G♯ major (eight sharps) and Beethoven, Sonata for Piano, Op. 13, second movement, measures 37–44, modulation from A♭ minor to E major, the enharmonic spelling of F♭ major (eight flats).

2. *Remote keys.*   A key other than a closely related key is known as a remote key.

In musical practice, modulations to closely related keys are more common than remote modulations. The closely related modulations to the dominant key and to the relative major or minor are the most frequent.

Assignment 1.1.   Write out, or name, the five closely related keys to each of the 15 major keys and 15 minor keys.

Methods of Progressing from One Key to Another

The following methods apply when modulating to closely related keys, as presented in this chapter, or to remote keys (Chapter 13).

a) *Common Chord* or *Pivot Chord Modulation.*   This is the most frequently used method of accomplishing a modulation. The modulation pivots around a chord which functions in the old and new keys simultaneously. Measures 1–2 of Figure 1.2 clearly outline the progression i-V⁷-i in G minor. If we play measures 2–4 only, the progression in these measures appears to be iv-V-i in D minor. The triad of measure 2 functions as i in G minor and as iv in D minor. It is the pivot chord, or the chord common to both keys.

Fig. 1.1.[2]

Mozart, Sonata in C Major for Piano, K. 545

In this type of modulation, the pivot chord is so located that the harmonic progression leading up to it and the harmonic progression in the new key beginning with the pivot are both normal progressions[3] in their respective keys (in Figure 1.1: G minor, i-V[7]-i; D minor, iv-V-i). Very often, as in Figure 1.1, the pivot is the chord immediately preceding the first V-I (or vii°-I) progression in the new key, though occasionally the pivot may be located two or even three chords ahead of this point. In Figure 1.2 the cadential progression ii°$_{6}^{5}$-V-i is so strong in D minor that the triad preceding this progression seems to be the logical location of the pivot.

Fig. 1.2.   Bach, *Herr Christ, der ein'ge Gotts Sohn*   (#303)[4]

---

[2] In this and subsequent figures, a single capital letter refers to a major key (D = D major) and a small letter refers to a minor key (b = B minor).

[3] Review *Elementary Harmony*, Table 14.1 and accompanying discussion. This table is repeated as Table 3.1 in the present volume. The terms "normal progressions" or "regular progressions" as used in these texts refer to chord progressions from this table.

[4] The number in parentheses refers to the number of the chorale in the collected editions of J. S. Bach's chorales, such as *The 371 Chorales of Johann Sebastian Bach*, edited, with English texts, by Frank D. Mainous and Robert W. Ottman (New York: Holt, Rinehart and Winston, Inc., 1966).

On other occasions, two or more chords may bear equal analysis as the pivot.

Fig. 1.3.

In this example, no matter which pair of chords is chosen as a pivot, the resulting progressions leading up to and away from the pivot are normal.[5] In analysis, usually only one pivot is indicated.

Each of the diatonic major and minor triads in a given key can be used as a pivot in modulating to closely related keys. Only infrequently, however, is the major dominant triad or the leading tone triad found as pivot. The dominant function is usually so strong in one key that it cannot easily assume a function in another key. The only frequent exception is in the modulation to the subdominant where the pivot I = V is usually immediately followed by V^7 in the new key.

Table 1.1 shows how each of the available diatonic triads in a key may function as a pivot to other closely related keys; this is illustrated in the keys of C major and C minor. Table 1.2 shows the pivot chords available for a modulation from a given key to each of its closely related keys, again illustrated in C major and C minor.

Assignment 1.2.   Name the available closely related keys to any chosen major or minor key when each diatonic triad of the original key is used as a pivot. Using Table 1.1. as a guide, spell each diatonic triad in the chosen key; for each triad indicate each possible use as a pivot chord and name the key to which each pivot progresses. For example, choose F♯ major and follow the list in Table 1.1.: I = VII in G♯ minor, I = VI in A♯ minor, I = IV in C♯ major, I = III in D♯ minor, ii = i in G♯ minor, ii = vi in B major, and so on.

---

[5]For an example from music literature, review *Elementary Harmony*, Figure 20.3 and accompanying discussion.

TABLE 1.1.

THE DIATONIC TRIAD AS PIVOT CHORD, ILLUSTRATED IN C MAJOR AND C MINOR

To Modulate from a Major Key		*To Modulate from a Minor Key*	
I (CEG)	= VII in D minor*	i (CE♭G)	= vi in E♭ major
	= VI in E minor		(vi-IV*; vi-ii$_6$)
	(VI-iv*; VI-ii$_6^{\circ}$)		= v in F minor**
	= V in F major		= iv in G minor
	= IV in G major		= iii in A♭ major
	= III in A minor*		(iii-vi*; iii-IV)
			= ii in B♭ major
ii (DFA)	= i in D minor		
	= vi in F major		
	= iv in A minor		
iii (EGB)	= ii in D minor**	III (E♭GB♭)	= I in E♭ major
	= i in E minor		= VII in F minor*
	= vi in G major		= VI in G minor
	= v in A minor* **		(VI-iv*; VI-ii$_6^{\circ}$)
			= IV in B♭ major
IV (FAC)	= III in D minor	iv (FA♭C)	= ii in E♭ major
	= I in F major		= i in F minor
	= VI in A minor		= vi in A♭ major
	(VI-iv*; VI-ii$_6^{\circ}$)		
		v (GB♭D)	= iii in E♭ major*
			= ii in F minor**
			= i in G minor
			= vi in B♭ major
vi (ACE)	= v in D minor**	VI (A♭CE♭)	= IV in E♭ major
	= iv in E minor		= III in F minor
	= iii in F major		(III-iv*; III-VI)
	(iii-vi*; iii-IV)		
	= ii in G major		
	= i in A minor		
		VII (B♭DF)	= IV in F minor**
			= III in G minor*

*These analyses are seldom used; the chord following this pivot (when using regular progressions) can also act as the pivot chord, as explained in Figure 1.3 and accompanying discussion. When a triad has two regular resolutions, one of which falls into this category, the two possibilities are indicated in parentheses.

**ii, IV, and v: (1) ii and IV in the new minor key contain the raised sixth scale step, which must be resolved upwards by step; (2) v in the minor key progresses best to VI, allowing the lowered seventh scale degree to resolve downwards.

TABLE 1.2.

AVAILABLE PIVOT CHORDS IN MODULATING TO A CLOSELY RELATED KEY

Modulation from a Major Key to its   *Modulation from a Minor Key to its*

Supertonic key   I = VII*
(C major–D minor)   ii = i
                        iii = ii**
                        IV = III
                        vi = v**

Mediant key   I = VI*   Mediant key   i = vi*
(C major–E minor)   iii = i   (C minor–E♭ major)   III = I
                        vi = iv   iv = ii
                                                              v = iii*
                                                              VI = IV

Subdominant key   I = V   Subdominant key   i = v**
(C major–F major)   ii = vi   (C minor–F minor)   III = VII*
                        IV = I   iv = i
                        vi = iii*   v = ii**
                                                              VI = III*
                                                              VII = IV**

Dominant key   I = IV   Dominant key   i = iv
(C major–G major)   iii = vi*   (C minor–G minor)   III = VI*
                        vi = ii   v = i
                                                              VII = III*

Submediant key   I = III*   Submediant key   i = iii*
(C major–A minor)   ii = iv   (C minor–A♭ major)   iv = vi
                        iii = v* **
                        IV = VI*
                        vi = i

                                         Subtonic key   i = ii
                                         (C minor–B♭ major)   III = IV
                                                              v = vi

* **See footnotes to Table 1.1.

b) Direct Modulation.   A direct modulation is one which is accomplished without benefit of a pivot chord. There are two varieties:

(1) Where the first chord of a phrase unmistakably functions in a key different from that of the cadence of the previous phrase. In Figure 1.4, phrase one begins and ends in D major; phrase two begins in B minor and remains in that key.

Fig. 1.4.   Bach, *Was mein Gott will* (#120)

D: vi   I₆   IV   I   I₆   I⁶₄   V   I b: i

V   VI   iv   i   V   i

(2) Where, during the course of the phrase, and at the point of modulation, there can be found one melodic line (any voice part) that proceeds by chromatically altered half step (two notes of different pitch with the same letter name). In Figure 1.5, the chromatically altered bass line, F-F♯, indicates the location of the direct modulation. Ordinarily, and as here, choice of any chord as pivot will result in an awkward harmonic progression.

Fig. 1.5.   Bach, *Jesu, der du meine Seele*   (#297)

B♭: I   I₆   V   g: V₆   i   iv₆   V

Terminology Variants

The terms "common chord" and "pivot chord" are standard. However, this type of modulation is often known as a *chromatic modulation* when the pivot chord is an altered chord in one or both keys. It is also known as an *enharmonic modulation* when the pivot chord is spelled one way in the original key and another in the new key, for example, Db F Ab = C♯ E♯ G♯. Common chord modulations making use of chromatically altered chords will be studied in Chapter 13.

The direct modulation is also known as a *phrase modulation* when a new phrase starts in a new key, or as a *chromatic modulation* when the new key is established within the phrase by a chromatic half step in one voice part.

A remote key is also known as a *foreign key, distant key,* or *extraneous key.*

Analysis of Modulations

When making a harmonic analysis which includes a modulation, use these models:

a) Common chord modulation.   Example: Mozart, Sonata, K. 545 (Figure 1.1)

$$\left| \ \text{g:} \quad \text{i } V^7 \ \right| \begin{array}{c} \text{i} = \\ \text{d:} \quad \text{iv} \end{array} \left| \ V \ \right| \ i \ V^7 \ | \ i$$

b) Direct modulation.   Example: Bach, Chorale #120 (Figure 1.4)

$$\left| \ \text{D:} \quad \text{vi} \ \right| \ I_6 \ IV \ I \ I_6 \ \left| \ \underset{4}{I_6} \ \underline{V \ I} \quad \text{b:} \quad i \ \right| \ V \ VI \ iv \ i \ \left| \ V \ i \ \right\|$$
cadence

Example: Bach, Chorale #297 (Figure 1.5)

$$\text{Bb:} \quad I \ I_6 \ \left| \ \begin{array}{l} V \\ \quad \text{g:} \quad V_6 \end{array} \ \right| \ i \ iv_6 \ V$$
bass: f-f♯

Assignment 1.3.   Make a harmonic analysis of these excerpts[6] as assigned.

---

[6]Measure 1 of any composition listed is the first complete measure. Repeats indicated by repeat signs and first endings are not numbered. In the Bach chorales, "phrase" refers to the music leading up to a cadence. Each verse (line) of the poem corresponds to a phrase; in editions without texts, these points are usually marked by a fermata. See *Elementary Harmony,* Chapter 13, footnote 3, for sources of excerpts used in these texts.

a) Bach chorales

No. 14, phrases 3 and 4
No. 38, phrases 3 through 6
No. 48, entire chorale
No. 51, phrase 1
No. 101, entire chorale
No. 140, entire chorale
No. 149, phrases 1 and 2
No. 167, phrases 1 through 3
No. 232, phrase 1
No. 268, phrase 1
No. 269, phrase 1 through 3

b) Instrumental music

Beethoven, Sonatas for Piano
   No. 2 (Op. 2, No. 2), third movement, Trio, measures 1–8
   No. 15 (Op. 28), second movement, measures 43–46
   No. 17 (Op. 31, No. 2), third movement, measures 31–35, 227–242

Mendelssohn, *Songs Without Words*
   No. 6 (Op. 19, No. 6), measures 12–17

Mozart, Sonatas for Piano
   A Major, K. 331, third movement, measures 1–8

Schumann, *Album for the Young*, Op. 68
   No. 7, all
   No. 29, measures 1–12
   No. 30, measures 17–24

APPLICATION

Written Materials

No new part-writing rules or procedures are necessary when writing a modulation.

A concise statement of the essentials of part-writing will be found in Appendix 1. For a more thorough review of the basic principles and reasons for formal part-writing procedures, review Chapter 6 of *Elementary Harmony: Theory and Practice,* second edition, and for amplification of the material of each specific rule, consult the index under "Part-writing" in that text.

Part-writing assignments in four voices, such as Assignment 1.4 below and similar assignments in the remaining chapters of this text, may be worked out in two ways other than that indicated:

1. For choral or instrumental performance. Review *Elementary Harmony: Theory and Practice,* pages 149–150. Appendix 2, "Instrumentation," in both that and the present text provides pertinent and specific information helpful in writing for instruments.

2. In open score. Write each voice on a separate staff, using the treble, alto, tenor, and bass clefs. Review *Elementary Harmony: Theory and Practice,* page 116.

Assignment 1.4. Part-writing.   Add alto and tenor voices. Make harmonic analysis, including location and type of modulation.

Assignment 1.5. Write the following chord progressions in four voices. Devise a satisfactory rhythmic pattern within each measure. Other keys may be used.

a) G minor. $\frac{3}{4}$ i | VI ii$_6^{\circ}$ V | i$_6$ iv = | i | VI ii$_6^{\circ}$ V | i ‖
$\phantom{a)\ G\ minor.\ \frac{3}{4}\ \ \ \ \ \ \ \ \ }{}_5^{}$

b) E♭ major. $\frac{4}{4}$ I iii IV V$_4$ | I$_6$ V$_6$ I = | | i ‖
$\phantom{b)\ E\flat\ major.\ \frac{4}{4}\ \ \ \ \ \ \ \ \ \ }{}_2$ ${}_5$ VI ii$_6^{\circ}$ i$_6$ V

c) F♯ major. $\begin{array}{l} 6 \\ 8 \end{array}$ I $\Big|$ ii$_4$ V$_6$ I I$_6$ $\Big|$ IV I$_6$ V I iii $\Big|$
$\qquad\qquad\quad\;\;$ $\;$2$\;$ 5 $\qquad\qquad$ 4

vi =
iv $\quad$ V$_4$ i$_6$ ii$^{\circ}_6$ V $\Big|$ i $\Big\|$
$\qquad$ 2 $\qquad$ 5

Melody Harmonization

To harmonize a phrase containing a modulation, follow this procedure:

1. Analyze the cadence. Is the cadence in a new key? Choose harmony for the cadence and write chord numbers below the staff.

2. If the phrase modulates, locate the pivot chord. Look for the first V-I progression in the new key, then look immediately ahead of this progression for the location of the pivot. Indicate the pivot below the staff.

3. Choose harmony for the remainder of the phrase.

4. Write the three lower voices, including non-harmonic tones where appropriate.

For an example, Figure 1.6 is an excerpt from Assignment 1.6, melody 6. It shows phrase 4, preceded by the final note of phrase 3. The cadence of phrase 3 is in A major, while the cadence of phrase 4 is in B minor. The entire last measure may be harmonized as V-i in B minor, so the pivot will be the last chord in the preceding measure (A: ii = b: i) leaving the first half of the measure to be harmonized as V-I in A major, as shown in the first analysis of Figure 1.6.

This simplest version may then be developed as in the next two analyses, or direct modulation to B minor or to D major may be used at the beginning of the phrase as shown in the remaining analyses. In most modulatory situations it is possible to find several different harmonizations; therefore, do not necessarily expect your first solution to be the most desirable one.

Fig. 1.6.

(*Fig. 1.6 continued*)

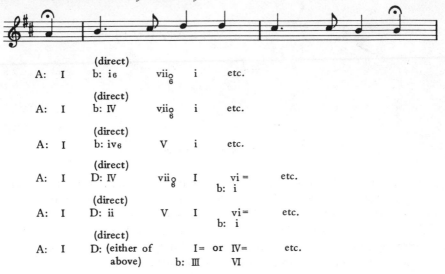

Assignment 1.6. Melody harmonization.   Harmonize melodies below, as assigned.

After completing your harmonization, it will be both interesting and instructive to compare your solution with that of Bach, as found in the 371 chorales. Where Bach has provided more than one harmonization,[7] study each one. (1) 102, (2) 236, (3) 95, (4) 120, (5) 340, (6) 153.

Assignment 1.7. Writing modulations.   Select an opening key, major or minor. From Table 1.2., choose a key relationship and one of the pairs of pivot chords indicated for that modulation; for example, E minor, modulation to the submediant, iv = vi. Write an example in four voices or for four instruments. Be sure that the original key is firmly established by at least one cadential progression, as in the examples in Assignment 1.5, and that the chords leading up to and away from the pivot chord are good acceptable progressions. Strive for a good soprano melody line.

Ear Training and Music Reading

Harmonic Dictation

Exercise 1.1. Harmonic dictation.   In taking harmonic dictation which includes modulation, it is usually not possible to hear the modulation until the pivot chord is passed. This is because the pivot chord functions in the old key; it sounds as a chord in the old key, and when the new key becomes apparent the pivot is no longer sounding. Follow these suggestions for listening to modulation, particularly when taking down chord numbers only (without staff notation).

a) Sing aloud or to yourself (as instructed) the tonic of the new key. Sing the tonic of the old key.

b) Compare the tonic of the new key with the tonic of the old key. The interval between the two tonic notes will indicate the location of the new key.

c) In subsequent hearings listen for a chord immediately preceding the first cadential progression in the new key—a chord which seems to function in both keys. This will be the pivot chord.

---

[7]Bach made as many as nine different harmonizations of some chorales. In the Mainous-Ottman edition, cross references to all the harmonizations are given with each chorale.

Self-Help in Harmonic Dictation

Under this heading will be listed hymn tune excerpts which can be used by students working in pairs to improve their ability in harmonic dictation. Each excerpt contains examples of the problem under current study and other previously studied theoretical devices. These excerpts are taken from two representative hymnbooks—

The Hymnal of the Protestant Episcopal Church in the United States of America, hereinafter abbreviated E.

The Methodist Hymnal, hereinafter abbreviated M.

Each excerpt is identified by its hymn tune name and the measure numbers from that hymn tune. For example, Southwell 5–8, M-284, means the hymn tune Southwell found in the *Methodist Hymnal* as number 284 (not page number), measures 5–8. See *Elementary Harmony: Theory and Practice,* page 152, for more complete details. From the same volume, see page 326 for hymn tune excerpts illustrating modulation from a major key to its dominant and from a minor key to its relative major.

St. Bride 5–8	M-51
Dominus Regit Me 5–6	M-67
Aus der tiefe 1–4	M-95
Southwell 5–8	M-284
Allgüter, mein Preis-	
gesang 7–8	M-285
Waits' Carol 9–12	M-377
Ratisbon 5–12	M-463
Du Friedensfürst, Herr	
Jesu Christ 9–12	M-491
Heinlein, all	E-55
O Traurigkeit, all	E-83
Veni Sancte, Spiritus, all	E-109
Luise 9–12	E-190
Oblation 9–14	E-205
Burford, all	E-410

Exercise 1.2. Writing a melody with modulation from dictation. The principles involved in harmonic and melodic analysis of modulation apply here also. Listen for the cadential progression in the new key and establish mentally the new tonic pitch. The interval relationship between the old and new tonic notes will indicate the name of the new key. Check this information against the name of the new key as found in writing the pitches by interval relationships.

Review *Elementary Harmony: Theory and Practice,* Chapter 20, "Melodic Dictation," page 327.

Sight Singing[8]

In singing a melody in which a modulation is involved, it is important to recognize the new key as soon as possible, since it is difficult to sing in one key while the music is written in another. Always look far enough ahead in the music while singing; when the new key becomes apparent, visualize the new tonic triad on the staff and establish its pitch in the mind. See page 87 of *Music for Sight Singing* for additional helps in singing modulations.

Keyboard Harmony

Exercise 1.3. Playing modulations to closely related keys at the keyboard. The ten progressions supplied for this exercise represent modulations to each closely related key from C major and C minor. In each, except as noted, the tonic triad of the old key is the pivot chord. In numbers 2, 3, 4, and 8, the tonic triad of the old key or the following triad may be considered the pivot chord.

a) Play each progression in all keys. Any progression may be played beginning with the first chord in a different soprano position—positions of following chords will be determined by basic part-writing procedures.

b) Modulate to a closely related key and return to the original key. For example, modulate from C major to the submediant and return to C major. Follow these steps.

    (1) modulate to the submediant (A minor) as in progression number 3.

    (2) determine relationship of new key (A minor) to original key (C major)—C major is the mediant of A minor,

    (3) from A minor, modulate to the mediant as in progression number 9.

To play a modulation from a major key to:	Play progression no.	Followed by progression no.
dominant and return	1	2
subdominant and return	2	1
submediant and return	3	9
supertonic and return	4	10
mediant and return	5	8

[8]The correlated studies in sight singing will be found in the author's *Music for Sight Singing,* 2nd ed. (Englewood Cliffs, N.J.: Prentice-Hall, Inc., 1967).

To play a modulation from a minor key to:	Play progression no.	Followed by progression no.
dominant and return	6	7
subdominant and return	7	6
submediant and return	8	5
mediant and return	9	3
subtonic and return	10	4

(1) to the dominant

I   IV   V   I   I =
                     IV   V   I

(2) to the subdominant

I   IV   V   I   I =   ii=
                     V   vi   IV   V   I

(3) to the submediant

I   IV   V   I   I =   IV=
                     III   VI   ii₀⁶   V   i

(4) to the supertonic

I   IV   V   I   I =   IV=
                     VII   III   iv   V   i

(10) to the subtonic
i
iv
V
i
i =
ii
vii$^o_6$
I

Exercise 1.4. Playing modulations to closely related keys. From Table 1.2, choose a key relationship and a pivot other than that used for Exercise 1.3. For example, modulate from C major to D minor, vi = v.

I
IV
V
I
I
vi =
v
VI
ii$^o{}^6_5$
V
i

Exercise 1.5. Play exercises from Assignment 1.4 at the keyboard.

Exercise 1.6. Melody harmonization. At the keyboard harmonize melodies as assigned from Chapters 10 and 15 from *Music for Sight Singing.* These will include modulation from a major key to its dominant key and from a minor key to its relative major, as studied in Chapter 20 of *Elementary Harmony: Theory and Practice.*

2

Binary and Ternary Forms

THEORY AND ANALYSIS

This chapter, the final one in our elementary study of small forms, is devoted to those structures now usually identified as *binary* and *ternary* forms, but which in the recent past have also been widely known as the *two-part song form* and the *three-part song form*. These new formal structures are presented here as were those forms presented in *Elementary Harmony;* that is, they are surveyed only in general terms with illustrations showing obvious examples. Detailed study of the more subtle manifestations of these forms, and study of still larger forms, such as rondo, sonata-allegro, etc., should be obtained in other courses and from textbooks designed for the purpose.[1]

The terms *binary* and *ternary* refer simply to formal structures that may be divided into two or three parts respectively. By this definition, forms already studied might be so identified; for example, a contrasting period would be binary as it is composed of two different phrases, or a phrase group made up of three phrases could be considered ternary. But the terms binary and ternary imply certain conditions which differentiate them from the forms already studied: (1) each part of a binary or ternary structure in itself consists of one of the smaller forms, such as period, phrase group, or double period; (2) the succession of parts is characterized by a relationship of keys, often tonic and dominant or tonic and relative major or minor (particularly true

---

[1] Walter Berry, *Form in Music* (Englewood Cliffs, N.J.: Prentice-Hall, Inc., 1966); Paul Fontaine *Basic Formal Structures in Music* (New York: Appleton-Century-Crofts, 1967); Douglass M. Green *Form in Tonal Music* (Holt, Rinehart and Winston, Inc., 1965). In addition to these recent texts the student should be acquainted with the old but reliable texts of Percy Goetschius, *The Homophonic Forms of Musical Composition* and *The Larger Forms of Musical Composition* (New York: G. Schirmer, 1898 and 1915), and their shortened version, *Lessons in Music Form* (Bryn Mawr, Pa.: Theodore Presser Co., 1932). As in other theoretical studies, it is to be expected that terminologies, definitions, and descriptions for the various formal structures will be found not to be standardized, resulting in inconsistencies when comparing like materials in various texts.

in ternary form); and (3) a definite contrast in the nature of the thematic material between the first and second parts, and in ternary form, a return to the original material in the third part.

Binary Form

Each of the two sections of binary form concludes with a strong cadence, usually perfect. The cadence of the first part may be in a closely related key. Each of the two parts will be any one of the smaller forms previously studied, very often the same in each part. At least one and usually both parts are larger than a phrase. Extensions will often be found, including (particularly in instrumental music) a prelude or introduction to the first part and a concluding section or codetta after the second part. One or both parts will often be set apart by repeat signs to emphasize the binary structure. In analysis, the two parts are often designated as A and B, where B indicates a contrast to A. Figure 2.1 could then be analyzed as   A   B , the small letters referring to phrases.   a a′ b c

Fig. 2.1.

PART I: Period, parallel

Etwas lebhaft   Schubert, *Die Forelle*, Op. 32[2]

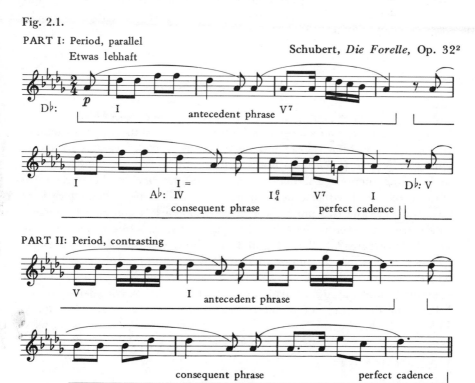

PART II: Period, contrasting

---

[2]In the original, the fourth phrase is repeated; this does not affect the analysis.

This example might appear to be a double period, especially if the cadence at the end of the second phrase is considered as a secondary dominant progression (V of V-V, or II-V) in the original key. But the principal characteristic of the double period is missing, that of the similarity between the first and third phrases.

Examples of binary forms displaying differing constructions within each part can be found in *Music for Sight Singing*, as follows:

MSS 289
>   First part: measures 1–12—period (two phrases, second with extension) ending with perfect cadence.
>   Second part: measures 13–34—double period (measures 13–24 and 25–34, each with extensions).

MSS 135
>   First part: measures 1–4—repeated phrase.
>   Second part: measures 5–12—period.

Assignment 2.1.   Copy melodies from *Music for Sight Singing* and make a formal analysis, as in Figure 2.1. Locate and describe any extensions. The first three of the following are regular (16-measure) binary forms without extensions. The rest are unidentified. 288, 430, 443; 165, 212, 220, 234, 294, 295, 317, 422, 432, 437, 444, 448.

Rounded Binary or Incipient Ternary

A formal structure, designated by theorists as either *rounded binary* or *incipient ternary*, exhibits characteristics of both two-part and three-part structures. It resembles the binary form just described as to cadences and structures within each part. It differs in that the final phrase of the period in Part II (or the final period of a double period) restates one of the phrases (or periods) of Part I, either exactly or in a modified form, a characteristic of ternary form. The two phrases (or periods) of Part II combine to make a single structure, even though the latter part of the structure is derived from Part I. In Figure 2.2, Parts I and II are both eight measures in length (periods), while the last phrase of Part II recalls the first phrase of Part I. The entire structure can be considered binary because the last two phrases combine to make an unmistakable period; it can also be considered ternary because of the return of material from Part I at the close. As binary, Figure 2.2 can be analyzed as $\|: A \quad : \|: B \quad : \|$, or as ternary,
$\qquad\qquad\qquad\qquad\qquad\qquad\qquad\qquad\quad a\ a' \quad\ \ b\ a''$

$$\|: A \quad : \|: B\ A\ : \|$$
$$\ \ a\ a' \quad\ \ b\ a''$$

Fig. 2.2.

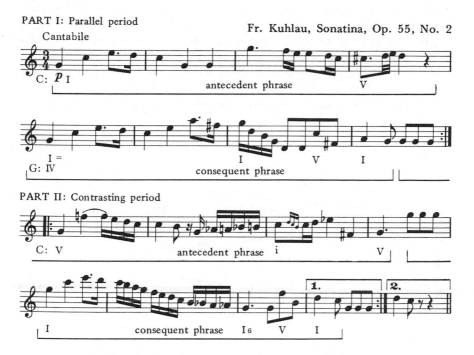

Assignment 2.2. Analyze the following rounded binary (incipient ternary) forms from *Music for Sight Singing:* 139, 198, 415, 417, 420, 438.

Ternary Form

In ternary form, the second part furnishes a contrast to the first part, while the third part is similar to, or even exactly the same as, the first part. It differs from the incipient ternary form in that the second and third parts are each unique structures and cannot be combined to comprise a single structure. The result is an ABA form; this three-part structure consisting of statement, contrast, and re-statement occurs with considerable frequency in all varieties of music, ranging from folksongs and popular songs to symphonic movements.

The *first part* of a ternary form may be any one of the smaller forms, usually larger than a phrase. It ends on a strong cadence in the tonic key or a closely related key.

The *second part* offers a contrast, usually by different thematic material, though at times by using material similar to the first part but in a related key. Any small form may be used and it usually ends on a weak cadence, often on the dominant, which serves as a bridge to the return of the original idea.

The *third part,* the return of the original idea, may be a literal repetition of the first part, either written out or indicated by a *da capo* (D.C.) at the end of the second part, or it may show strong similarity to the first part without being exactly the same.

Any of the parts may be found with extensions, codettas, or irregular phrase lengths.

Fig. 2.3.

PARTS I and III: Contrasting period   Gluck, *Orfeo*

PART II: Contrasting period

Melody number 282 from *Music for Sight Singing* displays a written third part.

First part: measures 1–8, a period ending with a perfect cadence in the key of the dominant.

Second part: measures 9–16, a period ending on the dominant note.

Third part: measures 17–24, a period ending with a perfect cadence in the tonic key.

In the example from Haydn, Figure 2.4, characteristics of both binary and ternary form appear. Structures such as this are identified either as *rounded binary*[3] or *ternary* depending on the authority quoted. The binary structure is obvious by the repeat bar lines and by the two strong cadences: in A major at measure 8 and in D major at the end. In analysis as rounded binary, measures 9–12, ending on the dominant, are explained as an extension or prolongation of the cadence on the dominant in measure 8. A diagram for the analysis as rounded binary for this example would be:

$$\| :A \quad : \| :B \quad : \| \ .$$
$$ab \longrightarrow \sim\sim\sim ac$$
$$\text{ext.}$$

From the ternary point of view, the material after the double bar includes both a phrase (measures 9–12) and a period (measures 13–20); these cannot be combined into one structure. With three distinct small structures including a return to opening material, the form is ternary:

$$\| :A \quad : \| :BA \quad : \|$$
$$ab \qquad c \ ad$$

Each analysis has its own merit and each is acceptable. The possibility of alternate analyses becomes particularly important in music where the formal structure does not readily fit standard definitions.

Fig. 2.4.

Haydn, Sonata in D Major for Piano

---
[3]Two different structures (review Figure 2.2) are identified as *rounded binary,* though not necessarily by any one given authority.

A smaller form incorporating the three-part idea is often known as a three part period. This consists of only three phrases, the first of which may or may not end with a strong cadence, and the third of which may or may not be written as a *da capo*.

Fig. 2.5.[4]   Schubert, *Die Schöne Müllerin,* "Wohin," Op. 25, No. 2

Assignment 2.3. Analysis of melodies in ternary form.   Copy melodies from *Music for Sight Singing* and make formal analysis. The first three of the following are regular ternary forms without extensions. In the others, any of the irregularities of phrase and period structure may be expected.   194, 268, 383; 115, 208, 274, 287, 309, 347, 351, 425.

---

[4]Repeated sections are written out in the original, and the opening measure of phrase 3 differs slightly in the repeat.

Assignment 2.4. Analysis of music compositions in any of the binary or ternary forms.

Beethoven, Sonatas for Piano

No. 1 (Op. 2, No. 1), second movement, measures 1–16
No. 2 (Op. 1, No. 2), second movement, measures 1–19
                          third movement, "Trio"
No. 11 (Op. 22), third movement, measures 1–30
No. 12 (Op. 26), first movement, measures 1–34
                          fourth movement, measures 1–28
No. 14 (Op. 27, No. 2), second movement, except "Trio"
                          second movement, "Trio" only

Mozart, Sonatas for Piano

F Major, K. 280, second movement, measures 1–24
D Major, K. 284, third movement, measures 1–17
C Major, K. 330, second movement, measures 1–20
A Major, K. 331, first movement, measures 1–18
A Minor, K. 310, third movement, measures 143–174
C Major, K. 545, third movement, measures 1–28

Chopin, Mazurkas

No. 24 (Op. 33, No. 3)

Schumann, *Album for the Young*, Op. 68

Nos. 3, 6, 8, 9

APPLICATION

Written Materials
Assignment 2.5.   *a*) Write original melodies in binary form using either regular phrase lengths only or extensions and irregular phrase lengths. Make a formal analysis of your melody as in Figure 2.1. Indicate tempo and dynamics.

b) Write original melodies in ternary form. Follow directions above.

Ear Training and Music Reading

Part III of *Music for Sight Singing* contains the remaining rhythmic and melodic materials to be completed during the present course of study. Since the theoretical materials of these seven chapters do not relate specifically to the harmonic materials presented in the remaining chapters of *Advanced Harmony,* the study of these seven chapters should be spaced evenly throughout the second-year theory program.

Rhythm

a) Triplet and Duplet Divisions in Chapter 18.

b) Changing Time Signatures and Less Common Time Signatures in Chapter 19.

c) Further Subdivision of the Beat in Chapter 20.

Each of these may be studied at a convenient time, preferably early in the course of study. Read carefully the introductory remarks to each chapter. The following applications of the study should be made.

a) Rhythmic reading from the chapters listed above.

b) Rhythmic dictation based on the problems presented in each of these chapters.

c) Use of these rhythmic patterns or metric schemes in assignments dealing with original composition.

Melody

a) Sight Singing from the chapters listed under Rhythm, above.

b) Melodic dictation incorporating these rhythmic patterns and metric schemes.

c) Modal Melodies in Chapter 17. Study of the modes is not proper to the study of harmony since they were little used during the historical periods under study. The ability to recognize and to perform in the modes should be prerequisite to studies in pre-seventeenth-century music and twentieth-century music.

d) Remote modulation in Chapter 21. Detailed consideration of this problem will be found in Chapter 13 of this volume.

3

Less Common Chord Progressions and Part-Writing Procedures

THEORY AND ANALYSIS[1]

Our study of chord succession so far has been concerned primarily with the "regular" or "normal" progressions, so called because of the frequency of their use in the music of the period under study. For review, these progressions are summarized in Table 3.1.[2] This table is valid not only for diatonic triads but also, with few exceptions, for seventh chords and altered chords built on the same roots.

TABLE 3.1.

THE COMMONLY USED CHORD PROGRESSIONS

I: I may progress to any other chord.
     Any chord may progress to I when I interrupts a progression listed in this table (e.g., ii-I-V)

ii: ii-V, ii-vii°

iii: iii-IV, iii-vi

IV: IV-ii, IV-V, IV-vii°, IV-I

V: V-vi, V-I

vi: vi-ii, vi-iii-IV, vi-IV, vi-V

vii°:   vii°-I, VII-III in minor

---

[1] Triad symbols for major keys will be used in the discussion of chord progressions, but will refer to both major and minor keys unless otherwise specified.
[2] Table 3.1 is taken from Chapter 14 (Table 14.1) of *Elementary Harmony: Theory and Practice*, where the derivation of the table is discussed.

Choice of the bass tone (root in bass or inversion) for each of these triads can be summarized as follows:

  a) Root in bass

    (1) I, iii, IV, V, and vi are commonly found with root in bass.

    (2) The supertonic minor triad (ii in both major and minor keys) is less often found with root in bass (first inversion is more common).

    (3) Diminished triads are rarely found with root in bass.

  b) First inversion

    (1) All diminished triads are usually in first inversion.

    (2) I, ii, IV, and V are commonly found in first inversion.

    (3) iii and vi are less commonly found in first inversion; these are used when the preceding bass note is the root of the triad (V-iii$_6$, I-vi$_6$).

  c) Second inversion.   The triad in second inversion is rarely used except in these special situations.

    (1) the cadential six-four chord

    (2) the passing six-four chord

    (3) the pedal six-four chord

    (4) the arpeggiated six-four chord

  d) Seventh chords.   Any seventh chord may commonly be found with any one of its members in the bass.

Common Exceptions

Progressions may also be considered regular when they appear in any of these situations.

  a) When triads in first inversion are found in succession and the bass is a scale-wise line. See also Figure 11.5 in *Elementary Harmony: Theory and Practice.*

Fig. 3.1.

Fig. 3.2. Bach, *Wie schön leuchtet der Morgenstern* (#323)

C: I_6 ii_5^6 iii_6 IV_6 V_5^6 I

b) In a harmonic sequence. The harmonic sequence can be identified by a regularly recurring pattern of *root* movements. Any chord progression which results is acceptable. In Figure 3.3, the roots move in the regularly recurring pattern, up a fourth, down a fifth, up a fourth, and so on:

| F | B♭ ↓ | E | A ↓ | D | G ↓ | C | F |
| I ↑ | IV ↓ | vii° ↑ | iii ↓ | vi ↑ | ii ↓ | V ↑ | I |

Fig. 3.3.

Schumann, *Albumblätter*, Op. 124, No. 4

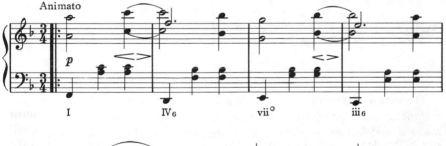

Animato

I   IV₆   vii°   iii₆

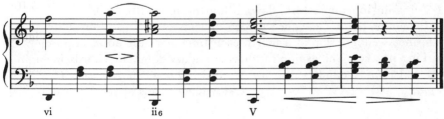

vi   ii₆   V

This sequence includes the progression vii°-iii, rarely found elsewhere, but common and acceptable in a sequence.

Roots of the chord need not be in the bass; the bass note pattern chosen for the first two chords is usually repeated as a melodic sequence, as in Figure 3.3 where the bass line consists of a root and a third of a triad in alternation. The resulting vii° triad with root in bass is acceptable because of the sequence, as would any bass position which might be unacceptable standing alone.

In a minor key, the natural form of the scale is ordinarily used during the sequence, with the resulting VII triad built on the lowered seventh scale degree. Figure 3.4 demonstrates the same series of root movements as in Figure 3.3 but in minor.[3]

Fig. 3.4.

Graun, *Der Tod Jesu*

(Slowly)

i   iv₆   VII   III₆   VI   ii°₆   V   i₆

The root movement pattern just described and illustrated is by far the most commonly used for a harmonic sequence. But any other regular pattern will make a satisfactory sequence, as in the first five chords of Figure 5.10: I-V-ii-vi-iii (roots up a fifth, down a fourth, up a fifth, etc.).[4]

In another harmonic sequence, roots down a second, up a fourth, in Figure 3.5, the ascending skip of a fourth each time gives the aural impression of V-I in a new key. This example utilizes secondary dominant chords, including the VII (V of III) and II[7] (V[7]of v) studied in *Elementary Harmony: Theory and Practice*[5] and the IV[7] (V[7]of VII).[6] The sequence ends at the VII triad.

---

[3]See also Figure 14.3 in *Elementary Harmony: Theory and Practice.*

[4]See also Figure 14.4 in *Elementary Harmony: Theory and Practice.*

[5]For VII, see page 261; for II (VofV), see pages 313ff.

[6]IV[7] is included in Chapter 8, "Secondary Dominant Chords." The symbol [d7] indicates a diminished seventh chord (a diminished triad above the root and a diminished seventh above the root). The vii[d7] is introduced in Chapter 5, "Diatonic Seventh Chords."

Fig. 3.5.   **Weber,** *Der Freischütz*

Harmonic sequences containing seventh chords and altered chords are by far more frequent than those using only triads. Such sequences are also frequently used as a means of modulating, as will be shown in Chapter 13.

c) When a passage includes a chromatic melodic line. The chromatic line (a line proceeding by half steps) usually appears in the bass but may be found in any voice. As might be surmised, the chord progression in this situation will usually include many altered chords; therefore detailed study will be deferred to a later chapter. Examples may be seen in Figures 10.22 and 10.23.

d) When a secondary dominant chord interrupts a normal progression. See Chapter 8.

Use of Less Common Progressions

No combination of two chords in succession is in itself unusable; examples of any possible chord progression can be found in music literature. But during the historical period under study (1650–1900) composers consistently used certain chord progressions (Table 3.1) more frequently than others. Those not listed there may be considered the less common progressions, although any of them can be very effective musically when used sparingly and judiciously. These less common progressions are summarized in Table 3.2.

TABLE 3.2.

LESS COMMON CHORD PROGRESSIONS

I: I between any pair of triads listed in this table, except after V or vii°.

ii: ii-iii, ii-IV, ii-vi

iii: iii-ii, iii-V, iii-vii°

(*Table 3.2 continued*)

IV: IV-iii, IV-vi

V: V-ii, V-iii, V-IV, V-vii°

vi: vi-iii (when iii is not followed by IV), vi-vii°

vii°: vii°-ii, vii°-iii, vii°-IV, vii°-V, vii°-vi

Although not every possible less common progression will be illustrated, the following points apply to any such usage:

a) the less common progression consists usually of two successive chords, though sometimes three or even four may be found.

b) in a less common progression, the soprano and bass are ordinarily found in oblique motion (Figure 3.6) or in contrary motion (Figure 3.7).

c) a less common progression rarely occurs more than once in a phrase of music.

Here are a few representative examples of these progressions:

Fig. 3.6. V-iii

Chopin, Nocturne, Op. 15, No. 3

Fig. 3.7. V-ii

Hymn: Gaudeamus Pariter

Fig. 3.8. vii₆°-vi

Hymn: Nassau

vii°₆-vi is a deceptive progression in which vii° substitutes for V.

Fig. 3.9. iv-III, repeated

Brahms, *Sankt Raphael*

Fig. 3.10. IV-vi

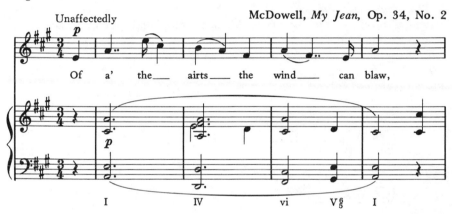

McDowell, *My Jean*, Op. 34, No. 2

Fig. 3.11. ii-vi-iii-V

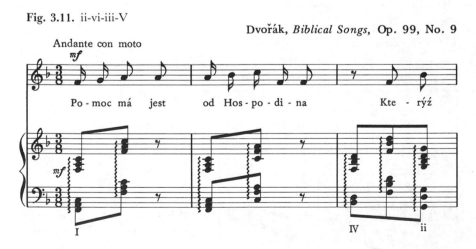

Dvořák, *Biblical Songs*, Op. 99, No. 9

The progression ii-vi (G B♭ D-D F A), coming as it does at the end of four measures, produces a temporary aural effect of a plagal cadence in D minor. The extension of the phrase for two more measures and the cadence at the end of the phrase establishes F major as the actual key.

Fig. 3.12. V-iii-ii

Reger, *Valet will ich dir geben*

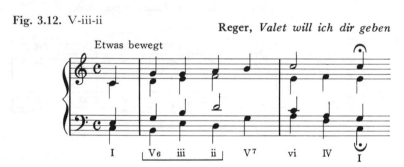

Fig. 3.13. VII-i

Brahms, *Von ewiger liebe*, Op. 43, No. 1

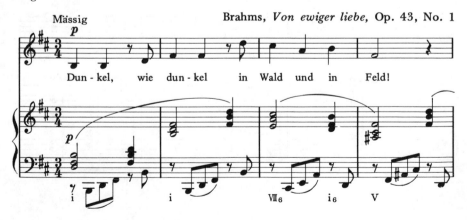

The VII triad in minor ordinarily progresses to III. This excerpt shows a rare use of VII$_6$ substituting for vii$_6^\circ$ between i and i$_6$.

Fig. 3.14. vi°-vii°

Bach, *Schwing dich auf zu deinem Gott* (♯ 142)

    i$_6$ vi$_6^\circ$ vii$_6^\circ$ i$_6$

The vi° triad is an occasional substitute for IV or ii in harmonizing the raised sixth scale step in minor. Here, successive first inversions produce the progression vi°-vii°.

Fig. 3.15. V and v   Haydn, Sonata in G Major for Piano

Trio

   g: i   V (v)   i

As will be recalled, the choice between V and v in a minor key is determined by the melodic direction of the seventh scale step at the appearance of the dominant chord. Should two lines each contain the seventh scale step, one ascending and one descending, a dominant triad with two thirds, one major and one minor, results. These two thirds are found no closer than the interval of a diminished octave.

In Figure 3.16, the dissonance is heightened still further by the addition of the tonic pedal tone.

Fig. 3.16. V and v   Bizet, *L'Arlésienne*, Suite No. 1, "Carillon"

Andantino

  c♯:   i   V (v)   i

Fig. 3.17.[7] Repetition of normal progression

Puccini, *La Bohème*, Act I I

---

[7]This figure also illustrates (a) a series of first inversions over a tonic pedal in measures 1–4; (b) the progression II-iii in measures 5–6 which can also be described as a deceptive resolution of the secondary dominant, discussed later in Chapter 8; and (c) the V[11], B (D♯) F♯ A C♯ E, at the final cadence, introduced later in Chapter 12.

In repeating any normal progression, a less common progression may result. Here the repetition of iii-vi-II (iii-vi-VofV) produces the less common progression II-iii (VofV-iii).

Fig. 3.18 V-IV, after a cadence

Mozart, *Haffner* Symphony, K. 385

When progressing from one phrase to another, especially after a half cadence, a less common progression may result. Here the final V triad of phrase one progresses to the opening IV triad of phrase two.

Assignment 3.1. Harmonic analysis. Identify examples of less common progressions in the following excerpts.

Bach: *371 Chorales*

    41, second phrase
    65, second phrase
    69, third phrase
    125, first phrase
    135, phrases one and two
    143, first phrase

Beethoven: Sonatas for Piano

    No. 7 (Op. 10, No. 3), third movement, measures 1–16; measure 10 = Vof vi.

Mozart, Sonatas for Piano

    C Major, K. 279, second movement, measures 1–6
    G Major, K. 283, first movement, measures 44–48
                    third movement, measures 172–195

F Major, K. 533, third movement, measures 95–102

C Major, K. 545, first movement, measures 18–26

Chopin, Mazurka No. 33 (Op. 56, No. 1), measures 16–20

Less Common Part-Writing Procedures

All the basic part-writing procedures, together with a number of commonly used exceptions, have now been studied. But it would be foolish to assume that composers of the past limited themselves to these basic procedures and exceptions. While it is true that these basic procedures account for most of the part-writing practices of composers, there are often musical situations which require special and sometimes unique approaches in accomplishing the composer's goal.

It would be virtually impossible to attempt to catalogue every deviation from common part-writing procedure and the reasons for such deviations. It can be said that, in general, such deviations are used to *improve* the quality of the four-part sound as a whole. "Violations" of part-writing rules are not to be used as an easy way out of part-writing difficulties; they should be used with discretion to make specific improvement in the part-writing texture.

Three deviations from the usual part-writing practices constitute the majority of less common procedures.

a) Unusual doubling—any doubling of any triad or seventh chord not listed under "Normal Doubling" in Appendix 1. For example, a major triad with one root, two thirds and one fifth when the root is in the bass.

b) Crossed voices—the normal pitch relationship of two voices is reversed. For example, the alto line may descend while the tenor is rising, with the result that the alto is lower than the tenor.

c) Abnormal distance between voices—more than an octave between soprano and alto, or between alto and tenor.

There are many reasons for the use of the above devices. A few are here illustrated and discussed.

a) To prevent octaves, fifths, or augmented seconds.

Fig. 3.19.

Allegro   Mozart, *The Magic Flute,* Act II

f Die Schön - heit und Weis - heit mit e - wig - er Kron!

At the sign (*), normal doubling (E♭ in tenor) would cause parallel fifths between tenor and alto in progressing to the following chord.

b) To prepare a suspension.

Fig. 3.20.

Mozart, *Requiem,* "Hostias et preces"

By doubling the third of the major triad at (*), the alto is in a position to prepare one suspension (of a double suspension) in the following measure.

    c) To change from close position (structure) to open position, or the reverse.

Fig. 3.21.

Bach, *Von Gott will ich nicht lassen* (# 191)

The triad with a doubled third, at *a*), is found between a triad in close position and a triad in open position. Open position is necessary at this point to separate the alto and tenor voices in the last half of the measure, and, since none of the options of Rule 7 is available, a triad early in the phrase must be chosen for unusual doubling. At *b*) is another example of a less common doubling to avoid parallel fifths, which would have occurred had the normal doubling B been found in the tenor.

d) For a sonority differing from normal.

Fig. 3.22.   Bach, *Jesus, meine Zuversicht* (♯ 338)

This chorale opens with a triad containing a doubled fifth. Because of the sustained A in the tenor, the accented passing tones G and E in the treble clef are much more effective. See also Figure 3.20 and the hymn, St. Catherine ("Faith of Our Fathers"), measure 4.

e) To add interest to the melodic line (or lines). This is probably the most important reason for the less common part-writing procedures. The use of unusual doublings, wide spacing of voices, and crossed voices often allows more interesting uses of non-harmonic tones. Such freedom will allow the use of two melodic lines in parallel thirds or sixths with each other, or two scale-wise lines in contrary motion to each other. Similarly, a single melodic line can be made more prominent by allowing it to progress scale-wise against a more steady background. There are many more possibilities in this category.

Fig. 3.23.   Handel, *Messiah*, "Let All the Angels
of God Worship Him"

Let all   the   an - gels of God.___ wor -   ship   Him.

At the sign (*), the alto leaps a fourth to double the third of the G major triad, putting the alto voice in a position to begin a descending scale-wise passage, which, at the end of the measure, descends to a point lower than the tenor voice. The tenor, in leaping to the G above the alto, introduces a suspension in measure 3.

In Figure 3.20, measure 2, first beat, the third of the V_6 triad is doubled in the tenor and bass, allowing the tenor to present a motive similar to the soprano line but in contrary motion to it.

Fig. 3.24.

Bach, *Sei Lob und Ehr dem höchsten Gut* **(# 248)**

At the sign (*), the alto leaps down to C instead of maintaining normal doubling of F, and begins a five-note ascending scale-wise passage, the first three notes of which are at the interval of a tenth with the bass part. Because of the effectiveness of this device, two part-writing irregularities at (*) can be overlooked. They are the excessive distance between soprano and alto and doubling of the third of the triad in tenor and bass. On the following beat (C major triad) a doubled third also occurs as a result of the alto line movement.

These and any other deviations from normal part-writing practices should be used sparingly and for *good musical reasons.* From this point on, the student may use more freedom in his part-writing efforts, but must be able to explain why his use of less common part-writing procedure improves the musical score he has written.

Assignment 3.2.   Study the following phrases from the Bach chorales. Write out, or be prepared to discuss, the location of less common part-writing practices and the reasons such devices are used. Also, locate similar situations in other chorales.

Chorale No. 18, last phrase   201, fourth phrase
             73, third phrase   207, first phrase
             99, first phrase   246, first phrase
             131, last phrase   254, first phrase
             167, first phrase   273, first phrase
             188, second phrase   280, first phrase

APPLICATION

Written Materials

The arranger or writer of music is constantly confronted with the problem of choosing effective chord progressions. He must determine whether the progression sounds well, not only by itself, but also in the context of the entire phrase of music. Experimentation with different chord progressions is highly desirable, so that the final choice is technically correct in addition to being musically interesting and aesthetically acceptable.

This process of experimentation, rejection, and acceptance plays a major part in the efforts of the composer. The music of any composer lives or dies according to the public acceptance or rejection of his choices. Since the chord choices indicated as regular progressions in this chapter are those which the accepted composers of the eighteenth and nineteenth centuries found most useful, they will also be most useful to the student at this time. The same is true of the "normal" part-writing procedures. However, the student is encouraged to experiment with the less common progressions and procedures, and to use them sparingly where they are musically effective. Results of such experimentation cannot be judged objectively, but only from the opinions of your teacher and other students, and from comparison of your work with that of the best composers of the period.

In working with less common devices in the following assignments, two basic principles should be kept in mind.

a) When using less common chord progressions, oblique or contrary motion between outside voices will help to insure a good aural effect.

b) Use less common part-writing procedures only to make specific improvement in the four-part texture.

Assignment 3.3.   Write the following progressions in four voices in keys as assigned. Chords may be used in inversion where desirable. Choose a time signature and create a rhythmic pattern which will insure acceptable harmonic rhythm.

I V iii ii V I V I	i iv III VI V i V i
I ii vi V I ii^7 V I	i v III iv i V i
I vii° vi ii iii IV I V I	i vi° vii° i i ii°^{7} V i

Assignment 3.4.   Harmonize melodies in four voices. Use examples of less common chord progressions and part-writing procedures where effective. Make harmonic analysis and edit the finished composition for tempo and dynamic markings. Melodies from Assignment 1.6 may also be used.

Assignment 3.5.   Write original exercises making use of less common progressions and part-writing procedures. Edit your composition and make harmonic analysis.

Ear Training and Music Reading

Exercise 3.1.   Harmonic dictation will now include examples of the less common progressions.

Self-Help in Harmonic Dictation

The following hymn tune excerpts contain examples of the less common progressions.

Innocents 1–2	M-61
Lenox 1–4, 9–15	M-100
Slane 1–4	M-256
Commandments 6–7	M-307
W Zlobie Lezy 9–14	M-396
Oldbridge 1–8	M-523
Bristol 5–8	E-7
Quem Pastores 9–16	E-35
Bedford 5–8	E-116
Selnecker 1–3	E-149
Praise the Lord 1–4	E-279
Windsor 1–2	E-284
Eudoxia, all	E-348
Culbach 1–2	E-373

Keyboard Harmony

Exercise 3.2.   Play chord progressions from Assignment 3.3 at the keyboard.
Exercise 3.3.   Play the following harmonic sequences at the keyboard in any major or minor key.

Fig. 3.25.

(a)

I   IV   vii°   iii   vi   ii   V   I

(b)

i   iv   VII   III   VI   ii°   V   i

(c)

I   I₆   IV   vii°₆   iii   vi₆   ii   V₆   I

(d)

i   III   iv   VII₆   III   VI₆   ii°   V₆   i

e) I IV₆ vii° iii₆ vi ii₆ V I

f) i iv₆ VII III₆ VI ii°₆ V i

g) I V ii vi iii IV V I

h) I iii ii IV iii V IV I ii₆ V I
      5

i)[8] i III₆ ii°₆ iv₆ III₆ v₆ iv₆ i₆ ii°₆ V i (also in major)
                                    4   5

j) ⌊I iii IV,⌋⌊ii IV V,⌋⌊iii V vi,⌋ IV V I

k) ⌊I IV vi,⌋⌊vii° iii V,⌋⌊vi ii IV,⌋ V I

l) ⌊i iv VI,⌋⌊VII III v,⌋⌊VI ii° iv,⌋ V i

---

[8]For soprano line, use scale steps 1-7-2-1-3-2 etc.

4

Application of Part-Writing Procedures
to Instrumental Writing[1]

THEORY AND ANALYSIS

In the study of part-writing, the four-voice chorale style[2] of writing has been used to illustrate procedures and to serve as a medium for student effort. There are, of course, many compositional styles other than the four-part vocal style, for example, piano solo, vocal or instrumental solo with accompaniment, three-part women's chorus, string quartet, and so on. The procedures already learned are, in general, applicable to any style of harmonic writing within the historical period under consideration. Exceptions will be found, as they were in four-part writing, while additional practices not in four-part writing will be found in other styles because of the characteristics of the instrument or voice for which the music is written.

The fact that instrumental styles of writing (in the historical period under study) are based on the principles of four-part vocal writing can be shown through the study of instrumental excerpts which follow. At the same time, these excerpts will also display writing techniques unique to instrumental writing, techniques made possible by the unique qualities of the instrument itself.

---

[1] Study of this chapter should be preceded by a review of *Elementary Harmony: Theory and Practice,* 2nd ed., pp. 299–305, "Writing Melody Harmonizations for Keyboard Performance."

[2] The meaning of the term "style" in reference to music is not constant. In the following paragraphs, style refers to various vocal and instrumental groupings, such as "piano style," "chorale style," and so on. For discussion of the various definitions of style see Willi Apel, *Harvard Dictionary of Music,* "Style" and "Style Analysis."

Similarities

In the following excerpts, applications of the principles of harmony and part-writing procedures (chord movement, doublings, use of non-harmonic tones, and so on) will be shown.

Although the first excerpt (Figure 4.1) appears to be in three voices, the inner voice actually functions as two voices by means of the arpeggio device.

Fig. 4.1.   Beethoven, Sonata for Piano, Op. 13,
second movement , meas. 1—4

Note carefully these details.

> measure 1, beat 1—major triad, normal doubling.
>> beat 2—V$_{\frac{4}{2}}$, no note doubled, the seventh in the bass resolves down normally in the next measure.
>
> measure 2, beat 1—major triad, first inversion, normal doubling (soprano doubled).
>> beat 2—another major triad in first inversion with normal doubling; the passing seventh resolves down normally.
>
> measure 3, beat 1—similar to previous measures.
>> beat 2—second half of beat (b♭dfa♭ chord) in which the seventh resolves normally, down by step.

Figure 4.2*a*) shows an excerpt in broken chord (Alberti bass) style while Figure 4.2*b*) shows the same music arranged in four-part vocal style. Study of Figure 4.2*b*) in comparison with 4.2*a*) will disclose the careful consideration given to voice leading when the chord progressions are written in instrumental style. Note also the use of correct doublings and resolutions.

> *a*) minor triad with doubled third, measures 1, 3.
> *b*) first inversion with doubled soprano, measure 1.
> *c*) no doubling of note of resolution when accented non-harmonic tones are used, measures 2, 5, 6.
> *d*) no note doubled and correct resolution of seventh in seventh chords, all of which are complete, measures 2, 4, 5.

Fig. 4.2.

Mozart, Sonata in C Major for Piano, K. 330,
first movement

Fig. 4.3.   Brahms, Intermezzo, Op. 116, No. 6

Even in a sonority as seemingly complex as that in Figure 4.3, analysis shows the harmonic progression and use of non-harmonic tones to be perfectly regular. This excerpt with the non-harmonic tones eliminated becomes the simple chord progression in Figure 4.4.

Fig. 4.4.

Differences

Extended Harmonies. In harmonic chorale style, chord changes are frequent, very often on each beat of the measure. In other styles, particularly instrumental, a single harmony is often of a longer duration, even for two measures or longer, as in Figure 4.5.

Fig. 4.5.

Brahms, Intermezzo, Op. 117, No. 1

Extended harmonies such as these are effective when written in conjunction with one or more of these features.

a) Striking melodic motive or theme (B. Op. 2, No. 1, first movement, measures 1–4)[3]

b) Strong rhythmic pattern (B. Op. 14, No. 2, "Scherzo," last 17 measures)

c) Change in inversion of chord during duration of single harmony (B. Op.7, third movement, measures 1–4)

d) In passages of rapid tempo (B. Op. 31, No. 2, last movement, measures 1–4)

e) Long melodic line implying a single harmony (M. Op. 53, No. 2, measures 1–2; also, Figure 4.5 above)

f) Melodic line in which the interest lies in the use of non-harmonic tones or chromatic scale passages (B. Op. 2, No. 2, fourth movement, measures 57–58)

g) In introductions, codettas, or cadenzas (B. Op. 7, first movement, measures 1–4; M. Op. 62, No. 4, measures 1–4 and last four measures)

Free Voicing.   In keyboard music, it is not necessary that a given number of voice lines be maintained throughout a composition. A glance at any keyboard composition of the eighteenth and nineteenth centuries will show a vertical texture of any number of voices from one to as many as eight or more, and a constant change in the number of voice lines as the composition progresses.

Fig. 4.6.   **Mozart, Sonata in B♭ Major for Piano, K. 281,**
third movement

Sonority Doubling.   Voice lines in keyboard music (as well as in orchestrations) are often doubled at the octave to produce a richer sound. At the keyboard, the octave naturally fits the hand position, so the device is used frequently in either or both hands. In instrumental ensemble music, two or

---

[3] In this section (*Differences*), musical excerpts cited but not quoted will be found in three sources: B—Beethoven, Sonatas for Piano; M—Mendelssohn, *Songs Without Words;* S—Schumann, *Album for the Young,* Op.68.

more different instruments may play in parallel unisons or octaves, producing a combined sound differing from that of any of the individual instruments.

A sonority doubling is always an octave reinforcement of a single voice line, such as a bass line or a soprano line. Octaves between two different voice lines can never be considered sonority doubling; these are simply undesirable parallel octaves.

a) Bass line doubled in octaves.

Fig. 4.7.   **Mozart, Sonata in F Major for Violin and Piano,
                                               K. 377, second movement**

b) Doubling in inner voices.

Fig. 4.8.

Andante   **Brahms, Romanze, Op. 118, No. 5**

c) Soprano voice doubled.

Fig. 4.9.

Arpeggiated Harmonies.   This very common device is used most often in piano music. It helps keep the music in motion when a single triad or a series of chords is being used. Almost any piano composition of the eighteenth and nineteenth centuries will provide an example of this device. The use of normal part-writing procedures in arpeggiated harmonies has been described in connection with Figure 4.2.

Pedal Point.   This device is common in instrumental music. Several varieties of the pedal point exist; these are among them.

a) Single pedal tone in the bass (see also Figure 4.18).

Fig. 4.10.

b) Double pedal in the bass, usually the interval of a fifth.

Fig. 4.11.

Schubert, Romanze

Andante con moto

Der Voll-mond strahlt auf Ber - ges-höhn wie hab ich dich ver - misst!

c) Inverted pedal (pedal in the upper voice).

Fig. 4.12.

Mozart, Sonata in F Major for Violin and Piano, K. 377, third movement

Tempo di minuetto, un poco allegretto

d) "Interrupted pedal," in which the pedal tone is repeated at frequent (and usually regular) intervals of time to help create the effect of a sustained pedal tone.

Fig. 4.13.

Bach, Prelude No. 2 in C Minor

For examples showing pedal points of longer duration, see

B. Op. 22, "Allegro con brio," measures 4–7;
M. Op. 19, No. 6, measures 7–14;
Op. 102, No. 3, last 12 measures (decorated pedal and inverted decorated pedal);
S. No. 31, measures 34–40;
No. 18, measures 1–4.
See also Chopin, Prelude, Op. 28, No. 15; the entire piece is built on a pedal tone
A♭ and G♯, alternating in the keys of D♭ major and C♯ minor.

Melody in a voice line other than the soprano. The melody line can be found
as an inner voice (see Figure 4.5), as the lowest voice line (Figure 4.14), or
can be divided between two voice lines (Figure 4.15).

Fig. 4.14.

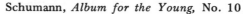

Schumann, *Album for the Young,* No. 10

Allegro animato

Fig. 4.15.

Beethoven, Sonata in C Minor for Piano,
Op. 13, first movement

Allegro di molto

Melody doubled in thirds or sixths.

a) Melody doubled at the tenth (an octave plus a third).

Fig. 4.16.   Mendelssohn, *Songs Without Words,* Op. 85,
No. 2

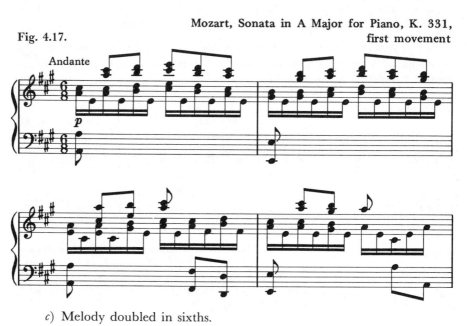

b) Melody doubled in thirds, plus additional sonority doubling.

Mozart, Sonata in A Major for Piano, K. 331,
Fig. 4.17.   first movement

c) Melody doubled in sixths.

Fig. 4.18.

Chopin, Mazurka, Op. 67, No. 3

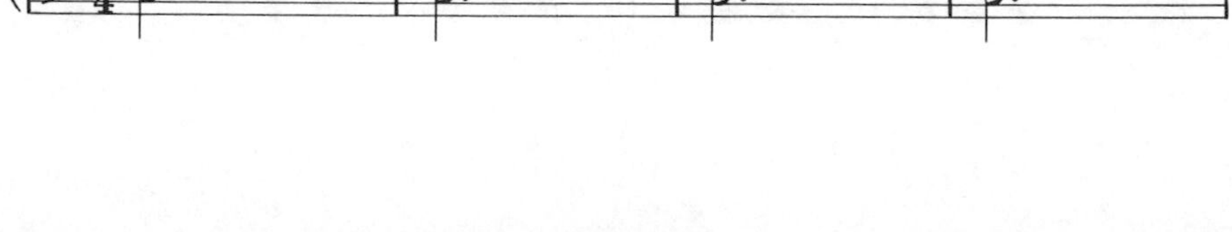

Range and spacing of voices.   In four-part chorale style, the upper and lower limits of each vocal line were determined by the average range of the human voice. Similarly, in instrumental music the range of the instrument determines the upper and lower limits of the music it plays. Most orchestral and band instruments have a much wider range than the human voice; the keyboard has a very wide range, allowing a melodic line to extend over a large compass.

Spacing between voices is often determined by technical limitations of the instrument. On the keyboard, for example, the two hands of the player are sometimes far apart, resulting in wide spacing between the inner voices. (See Figure 4.2, measures 3 to 6.)

A Note on Compositional Style

We have observed many times on previous pages that the harmonic concepts and part-writing procedures presented in this book are those of the historical period *c.* 1650–*c.* 1900. An analysis of almost any piece of music written in this period would show, in general, application of the materials thus far studied—principles of chord succession, use of non-harmonic tones, procedures of part-writing, principles of harmonic rhythm, and so on. For this reason, this historical era is often designated by the term, "common practice period." The question may then arise, why does not all the music of this period sound alike? Why does the music of Bach sound different from that of Mozart? Haydn different from Brahms? Schubert different from Berlioz?

Although all composers of this period generally made use of the same basic material, results from the pens of various composers differ because of the differing ways individual composers use given harmonic material and the frequency of use of one type of material in comparison with the frequency of use of other types. The following illustrations may clarify these two concepts.

a) Differing ways of using like harmonic material.   Compare the chorale excerpt in Figure 4.19 with the excerpt from Beethoven in Figure 4.15.

Fig. 4.19.

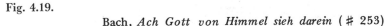

Bach, *Ach Gott von Himmel sieh darein* (# 253)

Both these excerpts use the triads i and V only, but note how differently they serve as a basis for musical composition. Bach uses one triad per melody note, alternating V and i; Beethoven uses each triad for four consecutive measures. Bach's bass line is melodic; Beethoven uses the same bass note for twelve measures. Bach's melody is always in the upper voice; in Beethoven, the melody alternates between soprano and bass, and has a much wider range. In Bach, the triad is stated simply and all notes simultaneously; in Beethoven the triad is divided and presented in broken chords.

Even the manner of presenting a simple arpeggiated triad can vary greatly with different composers as can be seen in the four excerpts of Figure 4.20, each for the left hand of the piano.

Fig. 4.20.

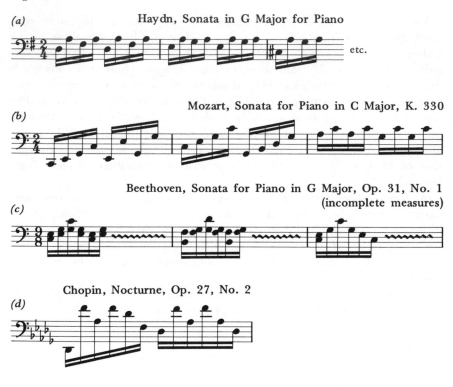

b) *Frequency of use of material.*   Inherent in the harmonic tonal system is such a great variety of harmonic, non-harmonic, melodic, and rhythmic possibilities that only by remote chance might two composers use the same theoretical material in the same way, or differing materials in the same proportions. Comparison could be made between a typical Bach chorale and a typical modern church hymn. Each is a succession of chords, usually with a chord change on each beat, but the hymn will contain only a few non-harmonic tones, while the Bach chorale will contain so many non-harmonic tones that each voice line almost becomes a melody itself. This difference in the frequency of use of non-harmonic tones is the major difference between the sound and effect of the two compositional styles. The excerpt from Brahms in Figure 4.3 displays a chorale-like chord progression. Yet it certainly does not sound like a typical chorale. The reason for the difference in sound becomes clear when it is observed that Brahms uses many multiple non-harmonic tones and that many of these occur on the strong part of the beat.

These contrasts illustrate the principle of difference of frequency of usage of any technical device. Similar comparison can be made between pieces of music on the basis of frequency of use of modulations, use of various triads, use of various seventh chords, of rhythmic patterns, and so on.

It is not the intention of this text to study specific stylistic differences between composers or between pieces of the same composer. The importance of the foregoing discussion is that the differing styles of various composers in the historical period under study are founded on the same basic materials—those which have been presented to this point, and those which will be found in the remainder of the volume. The student will be able, with this knowledge of technical materials and concept of stylistic differences, to make intelligent investigation of a given piece of music by observing what technical materials are used or omitted by the composer, observing the manner in which these materials are used and observing the frequency or infrequency of their use.

APPLICATION

Written Materials

Music Writing Projects[4]

To put into practical effect the principles outlined in this chapter, a series of writing projects will be presented, each including directions and explanations appropriate to the specific project. In subsequent chapters, applications of new principles and materials will be applied to projects similar to these, and the directions and explanations given here will also apply to such subsequent assignments.

---

[4]The projects presented here need not be completed before continuing with Chapter 5 and subsequent chapters. It is intended that work on these projects, and in Projects IV and V found in Chapter 5, be presented and/or continued throughout the remainder of the course at the instructor's discretion, using the new materials of each chapter in turn.

PROJECT I. *Realization of seventeenth- and eighteenth-century figured basses.* Figured bass is used almost universally today as an aid in teaching part-writing. Its original function was quite different. In music of the seventeenth and early eighteenth centuries which included a keyboard part (such as sonata for

Fig. 4.21.   **Handel, Sonata in G Minor for Violin and Figured Bass, Op. 1, No. 10**

Realization by Carl Friedberg, from G. F. Handel, *Six Sonatas for Violin and Piano,* copyright 1919 by Carl Fischer, Inc.

Realization by A. LeMaitre from Haendel, *Sonates pour Violon et Piano,* Paris. © Copyright Heugel et Cie. Permission granted by the publisher. Theodore Presser sole representative in the United States, Canada and Mexico.

Fig. 4.22.

Handel, Sonata in D Major for Violin and
Figured Bass, Op. 1, No. 13

Realization by A. LeMaitre from Haendel, *Sonates pour Violon et Piano*, Paris. Ⓒ Copyright Heugel et Cie. Permission granted by the publisher. Theodore Presser sole representative in the United States, Canada and Mexico.

Realization by Johann Hinnenthal from *Hallische Händel-Ausgabe*, Serie IV, Band 4, "Sechs Sonaten für Violine," Kassel, Bärenreiter-Verlag, 1955.

violin, flute, or oboe, song or aria with accompaniment, string trio with keyboard part, and so on), the keyboard part was written as a single melodic line in the bass, together with a figured bass. (This practice is also known as *thorough bass;* the bass melodic line is often termed *continuo.*) It was the responsibility of the keyboard player to *improvise* an accompaniment from this figured bass line. There is very little demand for such skill today; since about 1750, keyboard parts have been written out by the composer, and modern editions of earlier compositions supply a keyboard part based on the composer's bass line. Composing such a part is known as "realizing the figured bass." No two persons will realize a figured bass line in exactly the same way, since the figured bass does not indicate chord position or the character of any of the melodic lines above the bass. Figures 4.21*a* and 4.22*a* each show an excerpt from a violin sonata by Handel. Parts *b* and *c* of each figure show two different realizations of Handel's figured bass as found in current publications of these sonatas.

It is obvious from study of these two figures that various styles of keyboard writing can be employed in the realization. Note the simple use of block triads in Figures 4.21*b* and 4.22*b;* in Figure 4.21*c,* note the counter melody provided in the realization and in Figure 4.22*c* observe that the realization contains a melodic line when the solo plays a broken chord line (measures 1–2) and becomes chordal when the solo plays a melodic line (measures 3–4). Further ideas for the development of an accompaniment can be seen in Figure 4.23, where the given bass is doubled in thirds, and in Figure 4.24, which shows a four-part texture much like the four-voice chorale style.

Fig. 4.23.

Telemann, Partita 5

Fig. 4.24.   Lully, *Cadmus et Hermione* (1673)

Triads in the piano accompaniment for a solo voice or instrument are usually complete, even if this means the simultaneous use of the third of the triad or the leading tone in both the melody and the accompaniment (see Figure 4.23, measure 2, and Figure 4.24, measure 3). In a dominant seventh chord, the leading tone may be omitted in the accompaniment when it is found in the melody.

Any good pianistic device, as discussed in the earlier portion of this chapter, may be used in a realization. For further study of basic methods of realization, see the figured bass examples in the *Historical Anthology of Music,* Vol. 2, by Archibald T. Davison and Willi Apel (Cambridge, Massachusetts: Harvard University Press, 1950). To study realizations of greater complexity and more sophistication, consult collections of works by individual composers of the Baroque era, both in performing editions (such as those credited in Figure 4.21*b* and *c*) and in scholarly editions of complete works of these composers (such as credited in Figure 4.22*c*).

Assignment 4.1.   Copy this example on three staves, as in Figures 4.21–4.24, and write accompaniment on treble and bass staff, following the figured bass directions. The long line in the figured bass, as in measures 2 and 4, indicates the upper parts are to be held, or at least the same harmony to be maintained, while the bass moves.

Assignment 4.2.   In this example, much of the figured bass has not been indicated, on the assumption by the composer that the performer will understand from the context of the music what figured bass is required. In measure

3, below the C♯ is understood a "6"; the B natural is a passing tone, and below the A is understood a "7." In measure 18, and similar subsequent measures, a single triad per measure is appropriate above the florid bass line.

Assignment 4.3.

Bach, Sonata No. 1 in C Major for
Flute and Figured Bass

Assignment 4.4.   There is no figuration in the original.

Purcell, Song: *I Envy Not a Monarch's Fate*

I   en - vy   not_____ a   mon - arch's

Assignment 4.5. This figuration was supplied by the composer.

Handel, Italian Cantata No. 42: *Ninfe e pastori,*
"Ditele ch'il mio core"

Assignment 4.6. From *The Theater of Music,* a collection of songs published in London, 1685, by John Playford. No figuration was given by the composer.

William Turner (1651–1739), Song: *Ah Phyllis! Had You Never Loved*

soft— as   kind,   as   an - y   one   could— be;   Gods!

that that face should have a mind stain'd with in - con - stan - cy.

PROJECT II. *Harmonizing folksongs and traditional songs as vocal solo with accompaniment.* Harmonizing a folksong combines the skill of choosing a harmonic background for a melodic line, as studied throughout this course beginning with Chapter 10 of *Elementary Harmony: Theory and Practice,* and the skill of writing a piano accompaniment as just studied in Project I. Examples of this type of writing are to be found in the numerous collections of folk music readily available in most music libraries and stores. The student should play and sing many of these before doing any actual writing, thereby gaining an insight into the many and diverse ways of creating a good accompaniment.

The following collections of folksongs are particularly recommended because they include a large number of accompaniments from diverse geographical areas.

One Hundred Folk Songs of All Nations, edited by Granville Bantock, Bryn Mawr, Pa., Theodore Presser Co. Also in this series, other volumes containing folksongs of a single country, such as *One Hundred English Folk Songs,* edited by Cecil Sharp, *Sixty Folk Songs of France,* edited by Julien Tiersot, etc.

Das Lied der Volker, 13 volumes, edited by Heinrich Möller, Mainz, B. Schott's Söhne.

Brahms, Johannes, *48 German Folk Songs* and *28 German Folk Songs,* in volume 26 of the complete works of Brahms (Sämtliche Werke, Leipzig, Breitkopf & Härtel).

Botsford Collection of Folk Songs, 3 volumes, New York, G. Schirmer, Inc.

The following steps will be helpful in planning the harmonization.

a) Sing or play the melody; read the text carefully. Folksongs usually have no tempo indication; a tempo should be chosen appropriate to the character of the melody and the text.

b) Choose a harmonic progression, just as was done in harmonizing a chorale or a melody at the keyboard in earlier chapters. Be sure that each melody note is either part of a triad or a non-harmonic tone as previously defined.

c) Choose a style of accompaniment (arpeggiated, block chord, and so on) appropriate to the melody being harmonized. It is not necessary that the same style be maintained throughout the composition, but there should not be an abrupt change from one style to another.

d) Give special attention to the movement between the soprano and bass lines, just as in harmonizing a chorale.

e) Consider the possibility of adding a short (two- or four-measure) introduction and/or coda to your harmonization.

f) Edit your manuscript. This includes tempo markings, dynamic markings, and phrasing in the piano score. Phrasing marks are used to indicate melodic motives and places where *legato* is desired. Study Figure 4.25 and examples from published harmonizations.

Fig. 4.25.

Assignment 4.7.   Copy out melody or melodies, as assigned. Harmonize in instrumental style, complete with editorial markings.

(1)

English Melody, 16th century

Now, O now I needs must part, Part - ing though I
While I live I needs must love, Love lies not when

ab - sent mourn, Ab - sence can no joy im - part,
life is gone; Now at last, des - pair doth prove

Joy once fled can ne'er re - turn. Sad des-pair doth drive me hence,—
Love di - vi - ded, lov - eth none.

that— des - pair— un - kind - ness sends, If that part - ing

be of - fence, it is she— who then of - fends.

(2)

English Folksong

How plea - sant is it in the blos - som of the year to

stray and find a nook Where naught doth fill the hol - low

of the list' - ning ear, ex - cept the mur - m'ring brook or

bird in neigh - b'ring grove, that in sol - i - tude doth love to

breathe his lone - ly hymn. Lost in the min - gled song, I

care - less roam a - long from morn to twi - light dim.

(3)   **English Folksong**

A North Coun - try lass up to Lon - don did pass, Al -

though with her na - ture it did not a - gree, which___

made her re - pent, And so of - ten la - ment, Still___

wish - ing a - gain in the North for to be. O the

oak and the ash, and the bon - ny i - vy tree do___

flour - ish at home in my own coun - try.

(4)   **English Folksong**

Love me lit - tle, love me long,___ is the___ bur - den

of___ my___ song, Love that is too hot and strong___

burn - eth   soon   to   waste.   Still   I   would   not

have   thee   cold,   Nor   too   back - ward   nor   too   bold; _____

Love   that   last - eth   'till   'tis   old, ___   Fa - deth   not   in   haste.

English Folksong

(5)

Old   King   Cole   was   a   mer - ry   old ___   soul   and   a

mer - ry   old   soul   was   he;   And   he   call'd   for   his   pipe   and   he

call'd   for   his   bowl   and   he   call'd   for   his   fid - dlers ___   three.

Ev' - ry ___   fid - dler   he   had   a   fine ___   fid - dle,   A

ve - ry   fine ___   fid - dle   had ___   he,   then ___   twee, twee - dle   dee,   twee - dle

dee   went   the   fid - dler, And   so   mer - ry   we'll ___ all ___   be.

(8)   **German Folksong**

Es   blies__ ein__ Jä - ger wohl   in   sein__ Horn,   wohl

in   sein__ Horn,   und   al - les   was   er   blies__ das__

war__ ver - lorn.   Hol - lal - la,   tra - ra - ra - ra,   und

al - les   was   er   blies,   das__   war   ver - lorn.

PROJECT III. *Composing an original melody and accompaniment to a given text.* Composing an original song combines the skill of writing a good melodic line, as studied in previous chapters, and the ability to write an accompaniment, as studied in projects I and II. In addition, knowledge of combining a text with a melodic line is necessary.[5]

a) Meter. A poem, which, like music, has meter and rhythm, is usually chosen as a text for a song. The melodic line is composed with the metrical considerations of the poem in mind. Scansion of the poem is necessary to determine the accented and unaccented syllables of the poem; these will generally occur simultaneously with musical accents.

Sleep my child and peace at-tend thee,

All through the night.

Fig. 4.26.

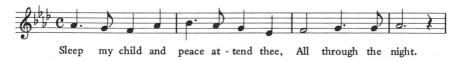

Sleep   my child and   peace at - tend thee,   All   through the night.

---

[5] See *Harvard Dictionary of Music,* "Text and Music."

Fig. 4.27.

The meter of a poetic line does not necessarily indicate a specific musical meter. In Figures 4.28 and 4.29 the same poetic lines have been set in both simple and compound time, but in both cases, the metrical accents of music and poetry coincide.

I walk in the gar-den ear-ly,

Just at the break of the day,

The flow-ers all whis-per to-geth-er,

Nev-er a word I say.[6]

Fig. 4.28.   Schumann, *Dichterliebe*, Op. 48, No. 12

----

[6]From *Am leuchtenden Sommermorgen* by Heinrich Heine; English translation of this and other German poems in this chapter are by Henry S. Drinker.

Fig. 4.29.

Franz, *Am leuchtenden Sommermorgen,*
Op. 11, No. 2

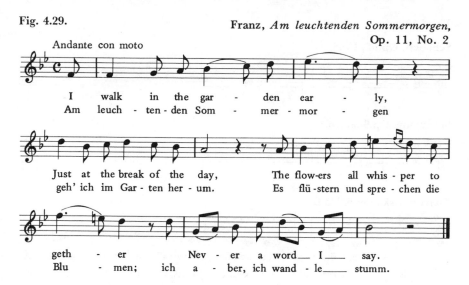

I walk in the gar - den ear - ly,
Am leuch - ten - den Som - mer - mor - gen

Just at the break of the day, The flow-ers all whis - per to
geh' ich im Gar - ten her - um. Es flü -stern und spre - chen die

geth - er Nev - er a word __ I __ say.
Blu - men; ich a - ber, ich wand - le __ stumm.

Figure 4.30 shows three settings of the same poem, each with a different time signature. The student should study the complete songs illustrated in Figures 4.26–4.30. For further study, the following poems have been set by two or more composers.

> *Die Lotusblume,* by Heinrich Heine
> > Franz, Op. 25, No. 1
> > Schumann, Op. 25, No. 7

> *Im wunderschönen Monat Mai,* by Heinrich Heine
> > Franz, Op. 25, No. 5
> > Schumann, Op. 48, No. 1

> *Er Ist's,* by Edouard Morïke
> > Schumann, Op. 79, No. 24
> > Wolf, *Morïke—Lieder,* No. 6

> *Minnelied,* by Ludwig Hölty
> > Schubert (Peters edition, Vol. 7, No. 3)
> > Brahms, Op. 71, No. 5

> *Mignon,* by Johann Wolfgang von Goethe
> > Schubert (Peters edition, Vol. 2, No. 68)
> > Shumann, Op. 79, No.29
> > Beethoven, Op. 75, No. 1
> > Wolf, *Goethe—Lieder,* No. 9

Fig. 4.30.

Schubert, Op.62, No.4

Schumann, Op.98a, No.3

Tschaikowski, Op.6, No.6

None but the ach - ing heart, knows all my an - guish! A -
Nur wer die Sehn - such kennt, weiss, was ich lei - de, al -

Schubert

Schumann

Tschaikowski

lone from joys a - part in grief I lan - guish.
lein und ab - ge - trennt von al - ler Freu - de

*At this point Schubert repeats the first four measures of the text with a different melodic line.

b) Form.   The form of a song is usually dictated by the form of the poem being set. In simple poetry, where the meter is constant and each line of equal length, a simple setting may result—one phrase of music (regular) for each line of poetry. Such well-known songs as "Auld Lang Syne" and "The Blue Bell of Scotland" illustrate this procedure. Any of the forms previously studied can be utilized: phrases, periods, double periods, and so on.

In addition, the devices of extension may be used. In Figure 4.31, part of the last line of the poetic stanza is repeated to extend the phrase.

Fig. 4.31.

Etwas bewegt

Schubert, *Frühlingstraum*, Op. 89, No. 11

I dreamt of the bright__ green mead - ow and
Ich träum - te von grü - nen Wie - sen von

thrush - es and ro - bins that sing,_____ and_____
lu - sti - gem Vo - gel ge - schrei,_____ von_____

thrush - es and ro - bins that sing.
lu - sti - gem Vo - gel ge - schrei.

In Figure 4.32, phrase 1, a short poetic line is extended to make a full four-measure musical phrase; in phrase 2, the same short line is extended to make a five-measure phrase.

Fig. 4.32.

The post brings you no note today,
my heart,
So now why act in this strange way,
my heart?

Etwas geschwind

Schubert, *Die Post*, Op. 89, No. 13

The post brings you no note to - day, my
Die Post bringt kei - nen Brief für dich, mein

heart,_____ my heart, _____ so now why act in
Herz,_____ mein Herz, _____ was drängst du denn so

this strange way, my heart, _____ my heart?_____
wun - der - lich, mein Herz, _____ mein Herz?_____

c) *Syllabic and Melismatic methods of text setting.*   When one syllable of the text is set to one note of the melody, the result is known as a *syllabic* setting. (See Figures 4.26–4.28.) When more than one note is assigned to a single syllable, the result is *melismatic,* and the group of single notes sung to a single syllable is called a *melisma.* Most art songs use syllabic settings with occasional short melismas, usually two or three notes, but sometimes longer, as in Figure 4.31.

d) *Strophic and through-composed songs.*   In the *strophic* songs, each stanza of the poem is sung to the same melody. Most church hymns are strophic. See also Schubert, *Die Schöne Müllerin,* Op. 25, Nos. 1, 7, 8, 9, 10, 13, 14, 16, 20. In the *through-composed* song, new music occurs in each stanza. Most art songs are through-composed.

e) *Vocal notation.*   The notation of the music of the vocal line differs from instrumental notation. When the setting is syllabic, notation of eighth notes and smaller are not "beamed"; each note carries its own separate flag.

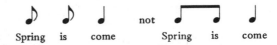

However, in a few very recent editions of music, the latter method can be found. In a melisma, the beam extends the length of the melisma (when eighth notes and shorter are used) and a phrase mark extends from the first to the last note of the melisma.

All these procedures are illustrated in the last four measures of Figure 4.31.

Assignment 4.8.   A number of poems are here provided to set to music with piano accompaniment. The student, if he wishes, may find other poems more to his liking. The finished composition should be fully edited, including tempo markings, phrasing, dynamic markings, and so on. Be sure to follow the procedures of vocal notation.

> Ye flowery banks o' bonny Doon,
> How can ye blume sae fair?
> How can ye chant, ye little birds,
> And I sae fu' of care?
>
> Thou'll break my heart, thou bonny bird,
> That sings upon the bough;
> Thou minds me o' the happy days,
> When my fause love was true.
>
> —*Robert Burns*

Of a' the airts the wind can blaw;
     I dearly like the west,
For there the bonnie lassy lives,
     The lassie I lo'e best:
There wild woods grow, and rivers row,
     And mony a hill between;
But day and night my fancy's flight
     Is ever wi' my Jean.

           —*Robert Burns*

The sun, above the mountain's head,
A freshening lustre mellow
Through all the long green fields has spread,
His first sweet evening yellow.

           —*William Wordsworth*

I dare not ask a kiss;
     I dare not beg a smile;
Lest having that or this,
     I might grow proud the while.

No, no, the utmost share
     Of my desire shall be
Only to kiss the air
     That lately kissed thee.

           —*Robert Herrick*

He that is down needs fear no fall,
     He that is low, no pride;
He that is humble ever shall
     Have God to be his guide.

I am content with what I have,
     Little it be or much:
And, Lord, contentment still I crave,
     Because thou savest such.

           —*John Bunyan*

Behold, a silly tender babe,
In freezing winter night,
In homely manger trembling lies—
Alas, a piteous sight!

The inns are full; no man will yield
This little pilgrim bed.
But forced he is with silly beasts
In crib to shroud his head.

With joy approach, O Christian wight,
Do homage to the King;
And highly praise his humble pomp,
Which he from heaven doth bring.

—*Robert Southwell*

The cuckoo is a witty bird,
        Arriving with the spring.
When summer suns are waning
        She spreadeth wide her wing.
She flies th'approaching winter,
        She hates the rain and snow;
Like her I would be singing,
Cuckoo - cuckoo - cuckoo!
        And off with her I'd go.

—*Anonymous, 17th Century*

Ask me no more where Jove bestows,
When June is past, the fading rose;
For in your beauties orient deep,
These flow'rs as in their causes sleep.

Ask me no more whither do stray
The golden atoms of the day;
For in pure love heaven did prepare
Those powders to enrich your hair.

Ask me no more where those stars light
That downwards fall in dead of night;
For in your eyes they sit, and there
Fixèd become as in their sphere.

—*Thomas Carew*

Sylvia, now your scorn give over,
Lest you lose a faithful lover.
If the humour you pursue,
Farewell love, and Sylvia too!

Long have I been unregarded,
Sighs and tears still unrewarded;
If this does with you agree,
Troth, good maiden, t'wont with me!

—*Anonymous, 16th Century*

Pack clouds away, and welcome day,
    With night we banish sorrow;
Sweet air, blow soft; mount, lark, aloft,
    To give my love good morrow.

Wings from the wind to please her mind,
    Notes from the lark I'll borrow:
Bird, prune thy wing, nightingale, sing,
    To give my love good morrow.

            —Thomas Heywood

Too late I stayed - forgive the crime;
    Unheeded flew the hours;
How noiseless falls the foot of Time,
    That only treads on flowers!

What eye with clear account remarks
    The ebbing of his glass,
When all its sands are diamond sparks,
    That dazzle as they pass!

Oh, who to sober measurement
    Time's happy swiftness brings,
When birds of Paradise have lent
    Their plumage for his wings!

            —William Robert Spencer

A wet sheet and a flowing sea,
    A wind that follows fast
And fills the white and rustling sail
    And bends the gallant mast;
And bends the gallant mast, my boys,
    While like the eagle free
Away the good ship flies, and leaves
    Old England on the lee.

There's tempest in yon hornèd moon,
    And lightning in yon cloud;
But hark the music, mariners!
    The wind is piping loud;
The wind is piping loud, my boys,
    The lightning flashes free—
While the hollow oak our palace is,
    Our heritage, the sea.

            —Allan Cunningham

My heart's in the Highlands, my heart is not here;
My heart's in the Highlands a-chasing the deer;
Chasing the wild deer, and following the roe,
My hearts in the Highlands wherever I go.
Farewell to the Highlands, farewell to the North,
The birthplace of valor, the country of worth;
Wherever I wander, wherever I rove,
The hills of the Highlands forever I love.

Farewell to the mountains high covered with snow;
Farewell to the straths and green valleys below;
Farewell to the forests and wild hanging woods;
Farewell to the torrents and loud-pouring floods.
My heart's in the Highlands, my heart is not here,
My heart's in the Highlands a-chasing the deer;
Chasing the wild deer, and following the roe,
My hearts in the Highlands, wherever I go.

—Robert Burns[7]

Away delights, go seek some other dwelling,
For I must die.
Farewell false love! thy tongue is ever telling
Lie after lie.
Forever let me rest now from thy smarts;
Alas, for pity, go
And fire their hearts
That have been hard to thee! Mine was not so.

—John Fletcher

Four ducks on a pond,
A grass-bank beyond,
A blue sky of spring,
White clouds on the wing:
What a little thing
To remember for years—
To remember with tears!

—William Allingham

Jenny kissed me when we met,
    Jumping from the chair she sat in,
Time, you thief! who love to get
    Sweets into your list, put that in.

---

[7] See setting by Schumann, *Hochländers Abschied,* Op. 25, No. 13.

Say I'm weary, say I'm sad;
Say that health and wealth have missed me;
Say I'm growing old, but add—
Jenny kissed me!

—*Leigh Hunt*

Keyboard Harmony

Exercise 4.1.   Assignments 4.1–4.6 may be played at the keyboard. Two students should participate, one to sing the melody or play it on an instrument, the other to play an accompaniment by realizing the figured bass.

5

Diatonic Seventh Chords

THEORY AND ANALYSIS

A seventh chord consists of a triad plus the interval of a seventh above the root.[1] Combining each of the four forms of the triad with each of the four varieties of the interval of the seventh (major, minor, diminished, or augmented) will produce a great variety of seventh chord structures. But when used as diatonic chords in a key, only the following will result:

Major-minor seventh chord

A major triad plus the
interval of a minor seventh
(G B D + G ↑ F = G B D F)

Minor-minor seventh chord
(Minor seventh chord)[2]

A minor triad plus the
interval of a minor seventh
(G B♭ D + G ↑ F = G B♭ D F)

Major-major seventh chord
(Major seventh chord)

A major triad plus the
interval of a major seventh
(G B D + G ↑ F♯ = G B D F♯)

Diminished-minor seventh chord
(Half diminished seventh chord)

A diminished triad plus the
interval of a minor seventh
(G B♭ D♭ + G ↑ F = G B♭ D♭ F)

Diminished-diminished seventh chord
(Diminished seventh chord)

A diminished triad plus the
interval of a diminished seventh
(G B♭ D♭ + G ↑ F♭ = G B♭ D♭ F♭)

---

[1] Review *Elementary Harmony: Theory and Practice,* Chapter 20, for the study of the major-minor seventh chord, the minor seventh chord, and the diminished-minor seventh chord, and their use as the V^7, ii^7, and $ii^{\circ 7}$ chords in a key.

[2] The abbreviated terminology in parentheses is more commonly used.

A seventh chord built upon each scale step will produce the following chord types and their identifying harmonic analysis symbols.[3] In minor keys, each chord may be found in two forms because of the alternate sixth and seventh scale steps; those not listed are not found with any degree of frequency.

	Major keys	*Minor keys*
Tonic seventh	Major seventh chord (I^7)	Minor seventh chord (i^7)
Supertonic seventh	Minor seventh chord (ii^7)	Half diminished seventh chord ($ii^{\circ 7}$)
Mediant seventh	Minor seventh chord (iii^7)	Major seventh chord (III^7)
Subdominant seventh	Major seventh chord (IV^7)	Minor seventh chord (iv^7) Major-minor seventh chord (IV^7)
Dominant seventh	Major-minor seventh chord (V^7)	Major-minor seventh chord (V^7)
Submediant seventh	Minor seventh chord (vi^7)	
lowered		Major seventh chord (VI^7)
raised		Half diminished seventh chord ($vi^{\circ 7}$)
Subtonic seventh		Major-minor seventh chord (VII^7)
Leading tone seventh	Half diminished seventh chord ($vii^{\circ 7}$)	Diminished seventh chord (vii^{d7})

Fig. 5.1.

(a) **Major keys**

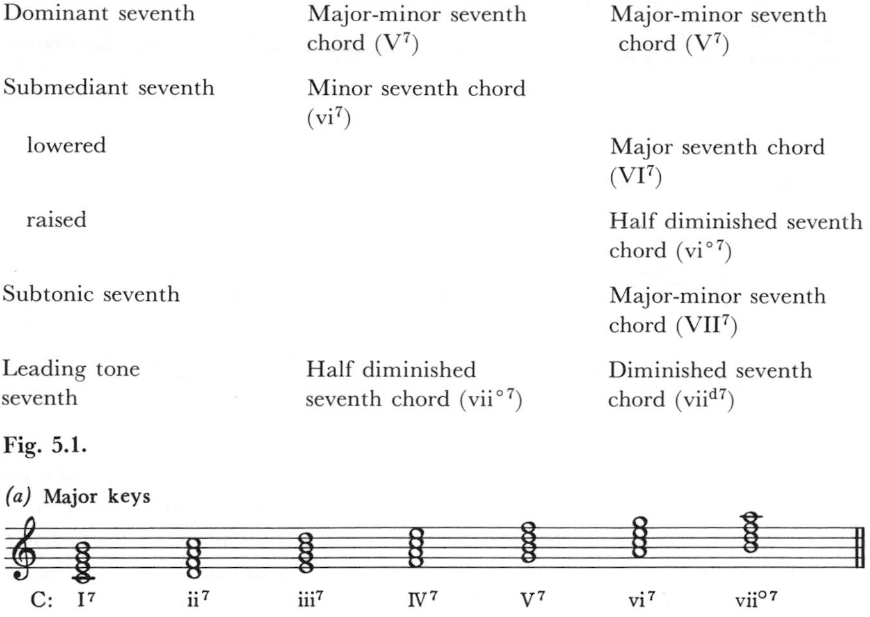

C: I^7 ii^7 iii^7 IV^7 V^7 vi^7 $vii^{\circ 7}$

(b) **Minor keys**

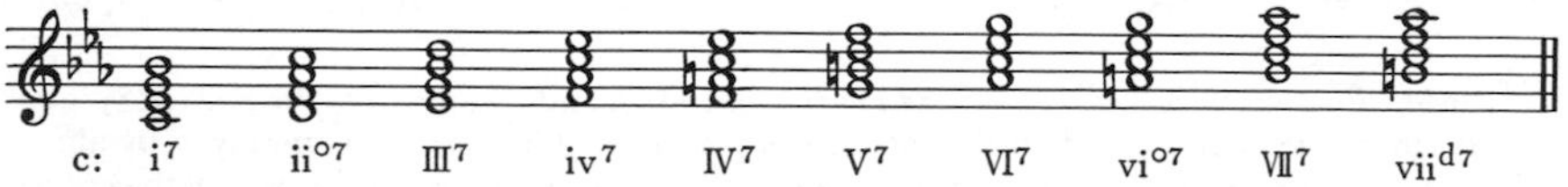

c: i^7 $ii^{\circ 7}$ III^7 iv^7 IV^7 V^7 VI^7 $vi^{\circ 7}$ VII^7 vii^{d7}

---

[3] The symbol "d7" in vii^{d7} indicates the quality of both the triad and the seventh: diminished triad and diminished seventh.

When found in inversion, the figured bass symbol for the inversion replaces the superscript "7", for example: IV^7, IV_6^5, IV_4^3, IV_2^4. The symbol "d7" is an exception: it should be retained when the symbol for inversion is used, for example, vii^{d7} and $vii^{d7}_6{}_5$.

Assignment 5.1.   Spell each of the above diatonic seventh chords in each major and minor key.

Seventh Chords in Sequence

Diatonic seventh chords are used frequently in the harmonic sequence, especially that based on a series of roots a fifth apart,[4] including all or part of the progression:

(Major) $I-IV^7-vii^{\circ 7}-iii^7-vi^7-ii^7-V7-I$
(Minor) $i-iv^7-VII^7-III^7-VI^7-ii^{\circ 7}-V^7-i$

In this progression, a chain of suspensions in each of two voices creates a seventh above each root. The seventh alternates between each of the two voices and in each case resolves to the third of the next chord. The sequence, as shown in Figure 5.2, could be extended by replacing the final I chord with a I^7 chord.

Fig. 5.2.

To extend the sequence in a minor key, v^7 is used instead of V^7 preceding the i^7 in order to prevent the melodic interval of the augmented second (see Figure 5.3, measure 2). Other than in this instance, the v^7 is rarely used.

This three-voice structure is shown clearly in the example from Telemann, Figure 5.3, measures 1–4 and 7–9, but observe the occasional omission of a bass tone, breaking the monotony of the regularly recurring interval. If, in measures 1–3, we supply the pitches A, F♯, and D respectively for each

---

[4] Review *Elementary Harmony: Theory and Practice,* page 188, and Chapter 3 of the present volume. The harmonic sequence based on the root movement of the fifth has been employed by almost all serious composers from the Baroque through the Romantic eras, and in the twentieth century, by many composers of popular music.

of the quarter rests, and in measures 7–9, we consider the half notes A and G as quarter notes, followed by D and C respectively, the sequence of roots in the bass becomes unbroken.

Fig. 5.3. Seventh chords in sequence

Telemann, Partita 5, "Aria 2"

In four voices with roots in the bass, seventh chords in succession are usually alternately complete and incomplete. Either the third or root may be doubled in the incomplete chord, except that the third should not be doubled in the V^7 at the cadence point.

Fig. 5.4. Bach *O Ewigkeit, du Donnerwort* (#26)

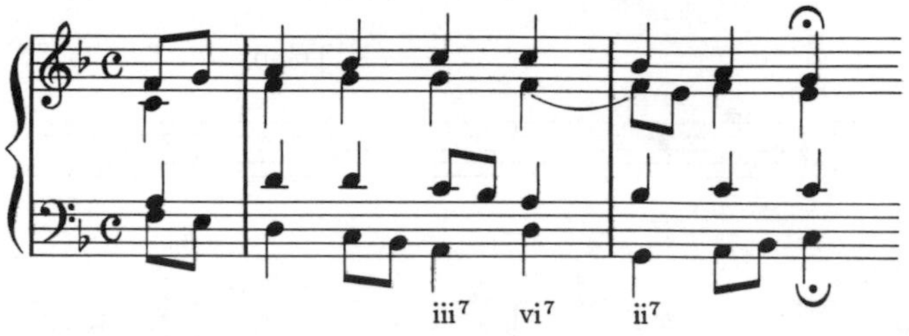

All seventh chords, whether used in a sequence or used singly, are commonly found in any inversion. In inversion, these chords are invariably complete. In Figure 5.5, root in bass alternates with fifth in bass in alternate seventh chords.

Fig. 5.5.

Poco più mosso — Grieg, *Holberg* Suite, "Musette"

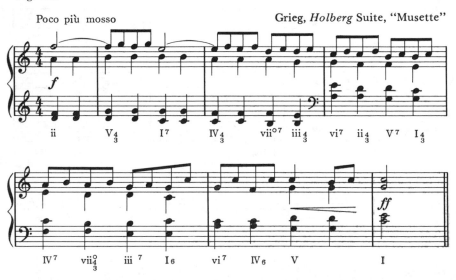

A sequence may consist of a pattern of root movements different from the one shown so far, and any sequence may be found with the seventh chord alternating with a triad. Both of these possibilities are shown in Figure 5.6, where the root movement describes the sequence, down a third and up a second, with alternating seventh chords and triads in first inversion.

Fig. 5.6.   Bach, Prelude in D Major (organ)

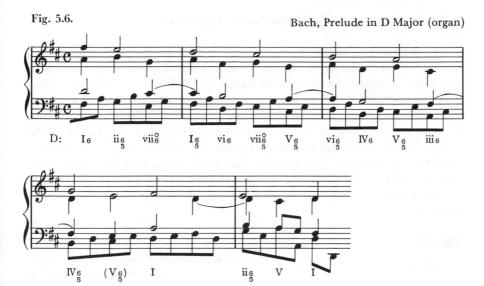

D: I₆ ii₆⁵ vii₆° I₆⁵ vi₆ vii₆°⁵ V₆⁵ vi₆⁵ IV₆ V₆⁵ iii₆

IV₆⁵ (V₆) I   ii₆⁵ V I

In instrumental style, there may seemingly be more freedom in the treatment of the seventh. In Figure 5.7, the circled sevenths resolve on the second eighth note following.

Fig. 5.7.[5]

Brahms, Ballade, Op. 118, No. 3

Allegro energico

g: V⁷ i   IV⁷ VII   I⁷ iv   VII⁷ III⁷ VI⁷

ii°⁷   V⁷   I

---

[5] I⁷ in a minor key (measure 2) is the secondary dominant of iv (V⁷ of iv).

The Sequence in Modulation

The sequence is valuable as a means of modulating. Any major-minor seventh chord in the sequence can become a dominant seventh chord or a secondary dominant seventh chord, usually II^7 (V^7 of V), in a new key. Also, any other seventh chord in the sequence may be altered to become one of the dominant seventh functions.[6] All these possibilities will allow modulation to many different keys, both closely related and remote. In Figure 5.8 at the *, A C E G (iii^7 in F major) is altered to become A C♯ E G (V^7 in D minor). Had the composer so desired, this same chord might have been used as a V^7 of V followed by V-i in G minor. Other possibilities, both in this sequence and the comparable one in minor, will suggest themselves to the student.

Fig. 5.8.

Alessandro Scarlatti, Concerto Grosso No. 3
for Strings and Continuo

---

[6] Any triad in the sequence can, of course, be treated in the same manner.

The seventh chord acting as pivot can also be diatonic in both keys, as in Figure 5.3, where iv[7] of E minor becomes i[7] of A minor.

The Single Diatonic Seventh Chord

Any diatonic seventh chord may be used individually rather than in a sequence as just shown. Each chord is ordinarily used in the same harmonic progressions as would the triad with the same root. Excerpts demonstrating representative uses of these chords follow. For an example of the progression IV[7]-VII, see Figure 3.5.

Fig. 5.9. I[7]

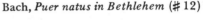

Bach, *Puer natus in Bethlehem* (# 12)

Fig. 5.10. IV[7], major key

Handel, *Messiah,* "Surely He Hath Borne Our Griefs"

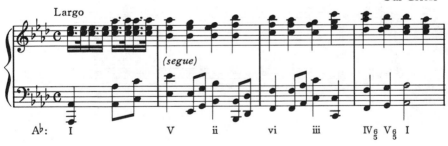

Fig. 5.11. iv⁷, minor key

Schumann, *Auf einer Burg*, Op. 39, No. 7

Fig. 5.12. IV⁷, minor key

Johann Crüger (1658), *Jesus, meine Zuversicht*

Fig. 5.13. vii°⁷

Reger, *Wie schön leucht't uns der Morgenstern*, Op. 135a, No. 28 (for organ)

Fig. 5.14. viiᵈ⁷

Bach, *Ist Gott mein Schild und Helfersmann*, (#122)

In the following figure, the octave D in the left hand is analyzed as a pedal point, the remaining notes producing the chord progression as shown.

Fig. 5.15. vii^{d7}

Chopin, Nocturne, Op. 37, No. 1

Lento sostenuto
p
3
i
vii d7
VI6
vii d7
i

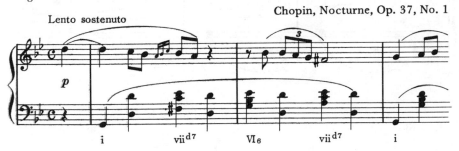

The use of vi°^{7} is limited almost exclusively to a context similar to that in Figure 5.16. The bass line progresses down by half step through the raised sixth scale step, at which point a vi°^{7} may be used. It may also occasionally be found in the harmonic sequence in place of VI^{7}, as in Figure 5.3, measure 4.

Fig. 5.16. vi°^{7}, minor key

Purcell, *Dido and Aeneas,* Act III

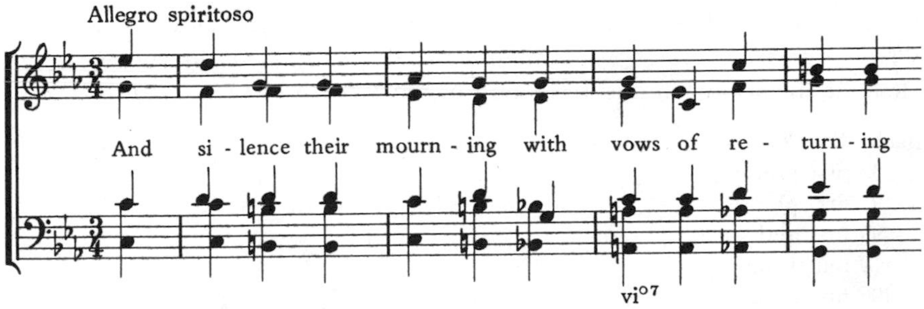

Allegro spiritoso
And si - lence their mourn - ing with vows of re - turn - ing
vi°7

At times a chord structure which appears to be a seventh chord may, on closer inspection, prove to be simply a triad with a non-harmonic tone incorporated in it. The C♯ of the "I^{7}" in Figure 5.17 is probably better analyzed as an accented lower neighbor tone, while the "iii^{7}" of Figure 5.18 is more likely a tonic triad with a suspension in the tenor voice and a retardation in the alto voice.

Fig. 5.17.

Faure, *Les Roses d'Ispahan,* Op. 39, No. 4

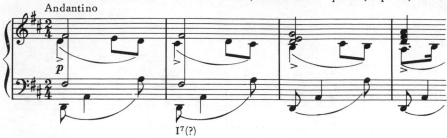

I⁷(?)

Brahms, *O Welt, ich muss dich lassen,*
Op. 122, No. 11

Fig. 5.18.

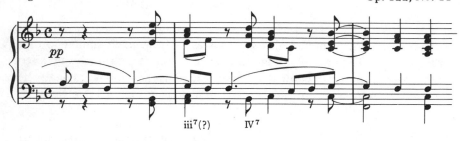

iii⁷(?)   IV⁷

Assignment 5.2. Harmonic analysis. Copy out excerpts below as assigned. Write in chord numbers below the bass staff. Identify non-harmonic tones. Describe the approach and resolution of the seventh of each seventh chord.

Bach: *371 Chorales*
  35 first phrase
  92 first phrase
  95 first and second phrases
  110 fourth phrase
  208 first phrase
  287 first phrase
  316 fourth phrase

Beethoven: Sonata for Piano No. 5 (Op. 10, No. 1), first movement, measures 1–22

Mozart: Sonatas for Piano

  F Major, K. 332, first movement, measures 58–67
  F Major, K. 533, third movement, measures 51–54

Schumann: *Album for the Young,* Op. 68

  No. 2, measures 17–20
  No. 43, measures 1–2

Murphy and Melcher, *Music for Study,* Chapters 16–17

APPLICATION

Written Materials

Procedures for writing the dominant seventh and supertonic seventh chords are equally valid for writing the remaining diatonic seventh chords. Particular attention must be paid to the introduction and resolution of the seventh, as described in Part-writing Rule 9.

These seventh chords are usually found complete, and in inversion they are almost invariably complete. When seventh chords with roots in bass are found in sequence, they are usually found alternately complete and incomplete. In constructing a sequence, roots in the bass a fifth apart, the incomplete chord will have either the third or seventh in the soprano. If the soprano is the third, either the root or the third may be doubled. If the soprano is the seventh, only the root is doubled. Each incomplete seventh chord in the sequence is found with the same doubling as the first incomplete seventh chord.

An exceptional part-writing procedure is necessary in the progression IV⁷-V when the seventh of the chord is above the third of the chord. In this position the resolution to V may easily produce parallel fifths as in Figure 5.19. (When the third of the chord is above the seventh, there is no particular problem.)

Fig. 5.19.

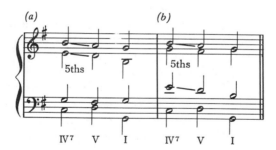

Several solutions are possible, including

Fig. 5.20.

Fig. 5.21.   Bach, *Nimm von uns* (#292)

The parallel fifth may also be avoided by progressing IV⁷-V⁷.

Fig. 5.22.   Hymn: Mendelssohn

The appoggiatura approach to the seventh, with the leap to the seventh in the same direction as the resolution, makes this solution less desirable. But the fault can be ameliorated by filling in the leap with a passing tone, as shown in Bach chorale number 47, fifth phrase.

Assignment 5.3.   Complete the exercises by filling in alto and tenor voices. Make harmonic analysis. Check each seventh chord to see that the seventh is correctly approached and resolved. Note that in most music, seventh chords are usually not so heavily concentrated as in the few measures of these exercises; they are heavily concentrated here to provide a maximum of part-writing experience. Overuse of seventh chords can produce a texture overly rich and even cloying; ordinarily, they should be sparingly used.

(1)

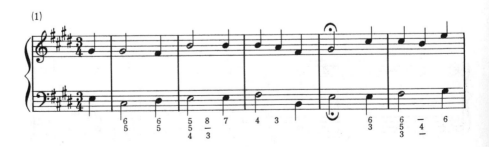

Music Writing Projects

PROJECT I. *Realization of figured basses.*
Assignment 5.4.   This is the first part of a binary form.

Assignment 5.5.

Bach, Sonata No. 1 in C Major for Flute and Figured Bass

PROJECT III. *Setting a text to music.*

Assignment 5.6. Using a poem found on pages 86–91 or a poem of your own choice, write an original song, using seventh chords as part of the harmonic texture.

PROJECT IV. *Original composition for piano solo.* In previous writing projects, one or more parts of the complete composition have been given. In this project, nothing is given; the student will be required to depend entirely upon his own originality in conjunction with musical knowledge previously acquired. The following steps may prove helpful.

a) Decide on a general mood or character for the composition—gay, sad, sprightly, contemplative, and so on. Choose an accompaniment style compatible with the character of the music.

b) Choose a form for the entire composition. The small forms are recommended for beginning work—double period, binary form, or ternary form. To this framework may be added introduction, coda, and interludes between periods or parts. Extensions within the phrase should also be considered.

c) When composing the melodic line, keep in mind the principles of good melodic writing already studied.

d) The harmony will depend upon the melodic line, so the melodic line should be composed with the harmony in mind. Occasional use of seventh chords and effective use of modulation will make your music more interesting.

e) A good composition is characterized by economy of melodic and rhythmic ideas. Rhythmic and melodic patterns throughout the piece should develop from those expressed in the first phrase of music. Avoid creating new rhythmic and melodic patterns and new accompaniment styles every few measures. Study the music in the volumes mentioned in *g*), below, to see how these composers maintain continuity with a minimum of rhythmic and melodic devices and accompaniment styles.

f) Do not necessarily be content with your first results. Go back over your work frequently to revise, polish, and improve. Remember that the greatest composers rarely achieved a finished work in the first writing.

g) The following works are recommended as good examples of piano writing in the small forms.

> Schumann, *Album for the Young*
> Mendelssohn, *Songs Without Words*
> Brahms, *Klavierstücke*

The Schumann pieces show easier styles of piano writing, especially numbers 1–3, 5. The Mendelssohn pieces are, on the whole, of moderate difficulty, with number 40 (Op. 85, No. 4) a good example. The Brahms pieces are the most difficult of this group.

Assignment 5.7.   Using one of the small forms, write an original composition for piano solo.

PROJECT V. *Original composition for solo instrument and piano accompaniment.* Writing for a solo instrument with accompaniment is very similar to writing for voice with accompaniment, with the following exceptions.

a) The instrumental solo line may have a much wider range, depending upon the range of the instrument itself.

b) The melodic line need not consist of as much scalewise movement as the vocal line. Skips, including extended arpeggios, are effective on many instruments. The characteristics of the instrument often determine what type of melodic line is possible or effective for it. For example, on the clarinet, many skips of a twelfth or larger are easy and sound well because of the finger placement on the keying mechanism; on the violin, double stops (two notes sounding simultaneously) can be played. The student should write at this time for his own instrument, or some instrument whose mechanics are somewhat familiar to him. There are many good books[7] on orchestration which give in detail the special characteristics of each instrument, including types of passages which are difficult or impossible. These should be consulted when writing for an unfamiliar instrument; even when writing for a familiar instrument, much helpful information can be obtained in this way.

c) When writing for an instrument, use correct clef and transposition. Consult Appendix 2 and, for more detail, any good orchestration text.

Assignment 5.8. Using one of the forms studied, write an original instrumental solo with piano accompaniment. Write for your own instrument or some instrument with which you are familiar. Edit your composition, including tempo and dynamic indications.

Ear Training

Exercise 5.1. *a*) Using any given note as root, sing the following seventh chords: major seventh chord, half-diminished seventh chord, diminished seventh chord. Sing with numbers (1-3-5-7) or with letter names.

Fig. 5.23.

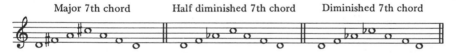

b) Same as *a*), using any given note as third, fifth, or seventh.

Exercise 5.2. Sing the tonic triad in a given key, followed by one of the seventh chords, as directed. Use letter names in singing.

I-I[7]	i-i[7]
I-iii[7]	i-iv[7]
I-IV[7]	i-IV[7]
I-vi[7]	i-VI[7]
I-vii°[7]	i-vii[d7]

Exercise 5.3. Sing a sequence of seventh chords in each major and minor key, singing from the root of each chord and using letter names.

Major: I-IV[7]-vii°[7]-iii[7]-vi[7]-ii[7]-V[7]-I
Minor: i-iv[7]-vii[d7]-III[7]-VI[7]-ii°[7]-V[7]-i

---

[7]For example, Kent Kennan, *The Technique of Orchestration,* 2nd ed. (Englewood Cliffs, N.J.: Prentice-Hall, Inc., 1970); Cecil Forsyth, *Orchestration* (New York: The Macmillan Co., 1949).

Exercise 5.4.   Sing the following chord progressions, using letter names, in various keys as directed.

Major keys	*Minor keys*
I IV^7 V I	i iv^7 V i
I I^7 IV V I	i IV^7 V i
I iii^7 vi ii V I	i vii^{d7} i
I vi^7 ii (or IV) V I	i VI^7 ii° (or iv) V i
I vii°^{7} I	i i^7 iv V i

Exercise 5.5.   Harmonic dictation will now include examples of all diatonic seventh chords.

Self-Help in Harmonic Dictation

The following hymn tune excerpts contain examples of seventh chords other than the dominant and supertonic sevenths.

New England 1–4	E-84
Garden 5–8	E-202
Richmond, all	E-319
St. Columbia 9–16	E-345
Wentworth 9–12	M-50
Stephanos 1–4	M-99
Gräfenburg 1–6	M-134
Mainzer 1–2	M-139
Blairgowrie 1–4	M-173
Barnabas 9–12	M-332
Manoah 1–4	M-403

Keyboard Harmony

Exercise 5.6.   Play the following progressions in keys as directed by instructor. The arabic numeral over the opening tonic triad indicates soprano note of the triad.

Major keys	*Minor keys*
1 or 5	1 or 5
I I^7 IV V (or vii$^\circ_6$) I	i i^7 iv V i
1 or 5	1
I I$_6$ IV V (or vii$^\circ_6$) I	i i$_6$ iv V i
$_5$	$_5$

$$1$$
$$\text{I} \quad \text{vi iii}^7 \text{ IV V I}$$

$$1 \text{ or } 5$$
$$\text{I} \quad \text{IV}^7 \text{ V I}$$

$$3$$
$$\text{I} \quad \text{IV}_6 \text{ V}_6 \text{ I}$$
$$\phantom{\text{I} \quad \text{IV}}_5 \phantom{\text{ V}}_5$$

$$5$$
$$\text{I} \quad \text{V}_6 \text{ vi}^7 \text{ ii}_4 \text{ V I}$$
$$\phantom{\text{I} \quad \text{V}_6 \text{ vi}^7 \text{ ii}}_3$$

$$5$$
$$\text{I} \quad \text{V vi}_4 \text{ ii}_6 \text{ V I}$$
$$\phantom{\text{I} \quad \text{V vi}}_2 \phantom{\text{ ii}}_5$$

$$1 \text{ or } 5$$
$$\text{I} \quad \text{vii}^{\circ}_4 \text{ I}_6 \text{ ii}_6 \text{ V I}$$
$$\phantom{\text{I} \quad \text{vii}^{\circ}}_3$$

$$1$$
$$\text{i} \quad \text{VI III}^7 \text{ iv V i}$$

$$1, 3, 5$$
$$\text{i} \quad \text{iv}^7 \text{ V i}$$

$$1, 3, 5$$
$$\text{i} \quad \text{IV}_6 \text{ V}_6 \text{ i}$$
$$\phantom{\text{i} \quad \text{IV}}_5 \phantom{\text{ V}}_5$$

$$3 \text{ or } 5$$
$$\text{i} \quad \text{v}_6 \text{ VI}^7 \text{ ii}^{\circ}_4 \text{ V i}$$
$$\phantom{\text{i} \quad \text{v}_6 \text{ VI}^7 \text{ ii}^{\circ}}_3$$

$$1 \text{ or } 5$$
$$\text{i} \quad \text{V VI}_4 \text{ ii}^{\circ}_6 \text{ V i}$$
$$\phantom{\text{i} \quad \text{V VI}}_2 \phantom{\text{ ii}^{\circ}}_5$$

$$1$$
$$\text{i} \quad \text{vii}^{\,d7}_4 \text{ i}_6 \text{ ii}^{\circ}_6 \text{ V i}$$
$$\phantom{\text{i} \quad \text{vii}^{\,d7}}_3$$

Exercise 5.7 Play the following exercises in keys as directed by the instructor.

$$\text{Major key: } 1$$
$$\text{I I}_6 \text{ IV}_4 \text{ vii}^{\circ}_6 \text{ iii}_4 \text{ vi}_6 \text{ ii V I}$$
$$\phantom{\text{I I}_6 \text{ IV}}_2 \phantom{\text{ vii}^{\circ}_6 \text{ iii}}_2$$

$$\text{Major key: } 5 \text{ or } 3$$
$$\text{I iii vi}^7 \text{ ii V I}_6 \text{ IV vii}^{\circ}_6 \text{ I}$$
$$\phantom{\text{I iii vi}^7 \text{ ii V I}}_5$$

$$\text{Minor key: } 1 \text{ or } 3$$
$$\text{i ii}^{\circ}_4 \text{ vii}^{d7} \text{ i ii}^{\circ}_4 \text{ V V}_6 \text{ i}$$
$$\phantom{\text{i ii}^{\circ}}_2 \phantom{\text{ vii}^{d7} \text{ i ii}^{\circ}}_3 \phantom{\text{ V V}}_5$$

$$\text{Major key: } 1$$
$$\text{I ii}_4 \text{ V}_6 \text{ I I}_6 \text{ IV vii}^{\circ}_6 \text{ I}_6 \text{ vi}^7 \text{ ii}_4 \text{ V}^7 \text{ I}$$
$$\phantom{\text{I ii}}_2 \phantom{\text{ V}}_5 \phantom{\text{ I I}}_5 \phantom{\text{ IV vii}^{\circ}}_5 \phantom{\text{ I}_6 \text{ vi}^7 \text{ ii}}_3$$

$$\text{Minor key: } 1$$
$$\text{i ii}^{\circ}_4 \text{ V}_6 \text{ i i}_6 \text{ iv vii}^{d7}_6 \text{ i}_6 \text{ VI}^7 \text{ ii}^{\circ}_4 \text{ V}^7 \text{ i}$$
$$\phantom{\text{i ii}^{\circ}}_2 \phantom{\text{ V}}_5 \phantom{\text{ i i}}_5 \phantom{\text{ iv vii}^{d7}}_5 \phantom{\text{ i}_6 \text{ VI}^7 \text{ ii}^{\circ}}_3$$

Exercise 5.8. Playing sequences of seventh chords.   Note that in minor keys the v^7 and VII^7 are used instead of V^7 and vii^{d7} until the cadence is reached, at which time one of the two latter chords will be used.

Continue each of the following exercises until the soprano has progressed to a note at least a fifth below its starting note. Finish the exercise with an authentic cadence. Play in any other key as directed. Each exercise is possible in major and minor, and in soprano positions as indicated.

Fig. 5.24.

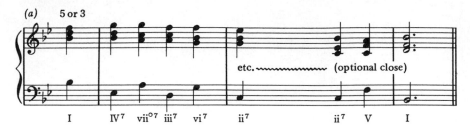

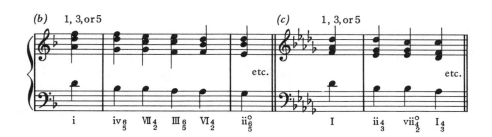

Exercise 5.9 Playing seventh chords from a figured bass.   This is an excerpt from the fifth movement ("Alla breve") of the Sonata in B minor for flute and continuo by Handel.

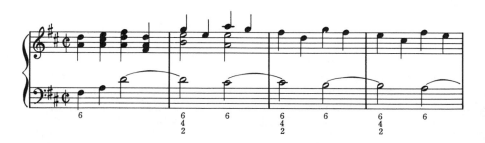

Assignments 5.4 and 5.5 may also be played at the keyboard. In these, two students should participate, one playing the melodic line, the other the accompaniment.

Exercise 5.10. Harmonizing a melody, including sequences. From *Music for Sight Singing*, harmonize melodies 91, 114, 139, 173, and 320, using a harmonic sequence in each. Depending on the nature of the melody, the sequence may consist of triads only, seventh chords only or alternating triads and seventh chords.

6

Introduction to Altered Chords

Chord members of the harmonic vocabulary may be divided into two groups—diatonic chords and altered chords. The diatonic chords (triads and seventh chords) have already been studied; they consist of chords that could be spelled by using scale tones only. This definition included the melodic form of the minor scale, resulting in the chords ii, IV, V, vi°, and vii°, each using either the raised sixth or the raised seventh degree of the minor scale.

Chords which display chromatic alteration of any scale step other than those of the melodic minor scale may be classified as altered chords. In the key of C major, D F♯ A is an altered chord since the fourth scale step, F, has been chromatically altered to F♯.

Chords are chromatically altered for a number of reasons, but in general, they enlarge the harmonic repertoire enabling the composer to give added variety to the harmonic sonority of the musical composition.

Figure 6.1 shows four altered chords in the key of E♭ major. First, the vii^{d7} follows an unaltered vii°^{7}. The use of this altered chord not only provides harmonic variety but also makes possible a more interesting melodic line in the soprano voice: C-C♭-B♭. Second, the progression I-i offers a feeling of temporary change of mode, major to minor. Third, the II^7 provides a sonority for the altered tone, A natural, in the melody, or conversely, it could be said that the use of this altered chord allows the presence of the A natural in the melody. Fourth, the II^7 is followed by still another alteration of the supertonic seventh, the ii°^{7}. In each altered chord, except the II^7, use of the unaltered chord, though less interesting, would have been correct.

Fig. 6.1.

Schubert, *Litanei*

What chord members may be altered, and to what extent may they be altered? In the practice of the seventeenth to nineteenth centuries, a chord is composed of major and minor thirds; a chord resulting from alteration of one or more of its members will remain composed of major and minor thirds, with the exception of a few chords containing the interval of the diminished third. The triad F♯ A C in C major is a distinct possibility, whereas F♭ A C is unlikely because of the interval of the augmented third, F♭-A. Not all possible altered chords built in major and minor thirds are used regularly; Figures 6.2–6.5 illustrate those which do enjoy some degree of usage. The diatonic triad or seventh chord is listed for each scale step in addition to the more usual alterations of these chords. The altered chords are divided, for ease of presentation, into five groups in the order in which they will be defined and explained in subsequent chapters.

The fact that a chord is altered does not usually cause it to be used differently in a chord progression. The altered chord will be preceded and followed by the same chords as would the unaltered chord (as shown in Table 3.1, Chapter 3). Exceptions to this statement will be illustrated and explained when the particular chord is presented in one of the following chapters. An unaltered chord followed by the same chord altered, or vice versa, can usually be considered a repetition of the same chord as far as harmonic progression is concerned.

Roman Numeral Identification

a) Any altered chord built in major and minor thirds with an *unaltered* scale step as root.

As with diatonic triads, the roman numeral will indicate the quality of the triad, for example:

$$\text{C major} \quad \begin{array}{l} \text{II} = \text{D F}\sharp\text{ A} \\ \text{ii}^\circ = \text{D F A}\flat \\ \text{iv} = \text{F A}\flat\text{ C} \end{array}$$

In almost all seventh chords, the seventh above the root is either diatonic in the key, indicated by the superscript ^{7}, or is at the interval of a diminished seventh above the root, in combination with a diminished triad, and indicated by the superscript ^{d7}.

$$\text{C major} \quad \begin{array}{l} \text{II}^7 = \text{D F}\sharp\text{ A C} \\ \text{ii}^{\circ 7} = \text{D F A}\flat\text{ C} \\ \text{vii}^{d7} = \text{B D F A}\flat \end{array}$$

In a few altered major-minor seventh chords, the seventh above the bass is chromatically lowered in relation to the key signature. The superscript $^{-7}$ indicates this alteration. All of these chords may use the alternate "V^{7}of" symbols.

$$\begin{array}{ll} \text{C major} & \text{I}^{-7} \text{ or V}^7\text{of IV} \quad \text{C E G B}\flat \\ \text{C minor} & \text{III}^{-7} \text{ or V}^7\text{of VI} \quad \text{E}\flat\text{ G B}\flat\text{ D}\flat \end{array}$$

The superscript $^{-7}$ is retained when the chord symbol indicates an inversion, for example: I^{-7}_6.

b) Any altered chord built in major and minor thirds with an *altered* scale step as root.

The altered root is indicated by placing a $\sharp$ or $\flat$ before the chord number; otherwise the chord symbol is written as above.

$$
\begin{array}{lll}
\text{C major} & \flat\text{II} & D\flat\ F\ A\flat \\
& \flat\text{iii} & E\flat\ G\flat\ B\flat \\
& \sharp\text{iv}° & F\sharp\ A\ C \\
& \sharp\text{vi}^{d7} & A\sharp\ C\sharp\ E\ G \\
& \flat\text{VI}^{-7} & A\flat\ C\ E\flat\ G\flat
\end{array}
$$

The signs $\sharp$ and $\flat$ do *not* precede symbols for chords built on the sixth and seventh scale steps in a minor key. As explained earlier,

VI = triad built on lowered sixth scale step
vi° = triad built on raised sixth scale step
VII = triad built on lowered seventh scale step
vii° = triad built on raised seventh scale step.

Other possibilities, such as a major triad on the raised sixth scale step, are very rare.

c) Triads built with intervals other than major and minor thirds. These triads, or seventh chords containing such a triad as root, third, and fifth, receive special numeral designations and will be described in Chapter 11. All are included in Group 5 in Figures 6.2–6.5.

Chord groups for Figures 6.2–6.5.

D—Diatonic chords
1—"Borrowed" chords, Chapter 7
2—Secondary Dominant chords, Chapter 8
3—Secondary Leading Tone chords, Chapter 9
4—Augmented Triads and the Neapolitan Sixth chord, Chapter 10
5—Augmented Sixth chords, Chapter 11

Fig. 6.2. Altered Triads: Major Keys

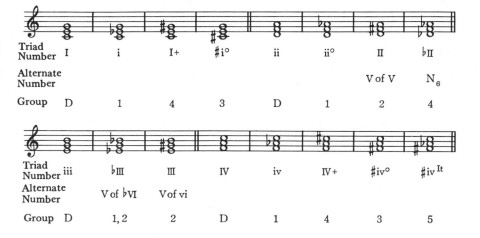

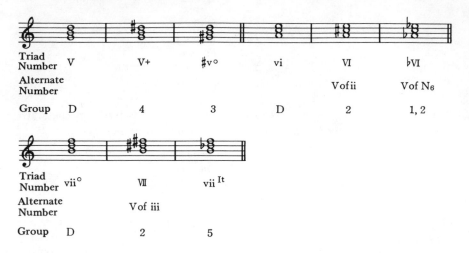

Triad Number	V	V+	♯v°	vi	VI	♭VI
Alternate Number					V of ii	V of N₆
Group	D	4	3	D	2	1, 2

Triad Number	vii°	VII	vii It
Alternate Number		V of iii	
Group	D	2	5

Fig. 6.3. Altered Triads: Minor Keys

Triad Number	i	I	ii°	II	♭II	III	III+
Alternate Number		V of iv		V of V	N₆	V of VI	
Group	D	D, 2	D, 3	2	4	D	4

Triad Number	iv	IV	♯iv°	♯iv It	v	V
Alternate Number		V of VII				
Group	D	D, 2	3	5	D	D

Triad Number	VI	vi°	VII	vii°
Alternate Number	V of N₆		V of III	
Group	D, 2	3	D, 2	D

Fig. 6.4. Altered Seventh Chords: Major Keys

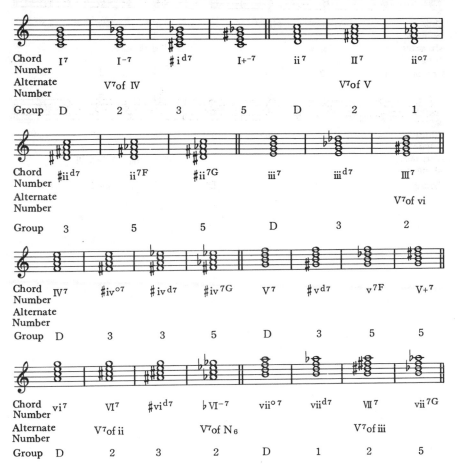

Fig. 6.5. Altered Seventh Chords: Minor Keys

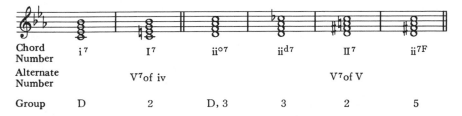

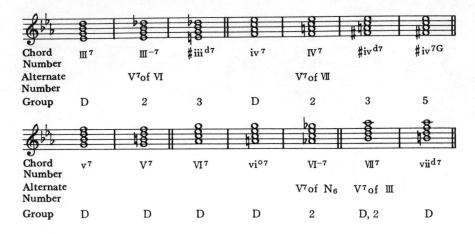

Chord Number	III^7	III^{-7}	$\#iii^{d7}$	iv^7	IV^7	$\#iv^{d7}$	$\#iv^{7}G$
Alternate Number		$V^7$of VI			$V^7$of VII		
Group	D	2	3	D	2	3	5

Chord Number	v^7	V^7	VI^7	vi^{o7}	VI^{-7}	VII^7	vii^{d7}
Alternate Number					$V^7$of N_6	$V^7$of III	
Group	D	D	D	D	2	D, 2	D

7

Borrowed Chords

The chords of Figure 7.1 (Group 1 in Figures 6.2 and 6.4) contain chromatic alterations when found in a major key, but are diatonic when found in a minor key. For example, D F A♭ in C major is an altered triad, displaying the altered sixth scale step A♭, while in C minor it is a diatonic triad. These chords are not literally borrowed from a minor key, but the term "borrowed chords" conveniently describes them. Each borrowed chord contains one or both of the lowered third, sixth, and seventh scale steps, these being characteristic of the minor scale.

Fig. 7.1.

C: i   ii°   ♭III   iv   ♭VI   ii°7   viid7

Assignment 7.1. Spell each of the borrowed chords shown in Figure 7.1 in each major key.

A borrowed chord may be introduced by its diatonic (unaltered) version or it may appear independent of its diatonic counterpart. In Figure 7.2, we find an example of the first of these possibilities, where IV (B♭ D F) progresses to iv (B♭ D♭ F). Because of the very slow tempo, the chord on the following eighth note could be considered as a ii° (G B♭ D♭).

Fig. 7.2. iv, ii°

Schubert, *Das Wirtshaus*, Op. 89, No. 21

Figure 6.1 contains two additional progressions of this type: $\text{vii}^\circ_4{}^3$-$\text{vii}^{d7}_4{}^3$ and I_6-i_6.

Borrowed chords introduced independently of the parallel major chord are shown in Figures 7.3–7.10.

Fig. 7.3. ii°⁷, iv

Fauré, *Lydia*, Op. 4, No. 2

In Figure 7.4, following the ♭VI is a iv$_6$ created by the passing tone figure G♭-A♭-B♭ in the tenor voice. The music for Piano I is omitted in this illustration.

Fig. 7.4. ♭VI

Brahms, *Liebeslieder Walzer,* Op. 52

The ♭VI is used as a deceptive cadence in Figure 7.5. The phrase following the cadence begins with a direct modulation employing a diminished seventh chord, thereby eliminating the necessity for resolution of the ♭VI.

Fig. 7.5. ♭VI

Bach, *Vater unser im Himmelreich* (#267)

vi   ii⁶₅ V ♭VI

The vii^{d7} of Figure 7.6 sounds over a tonic pedal: C♯ E G B♭ over D.

Fig. 7.6. vii^{d7}

Haydn, Sonata in D Major for Piano

Temporary Change of Mode

   Closely related to the principle of the borrowed chord is that of the temporary change of mode in a composition, when one or more chords or a few measures of music may be found in the mode (major or minor) opposite to that of most of the composition. This feeling of change of mode can be accomplished in two ways: (1) by an occasional interpolation of the minor tonic triad as in Figure 7.7, or (2) by a series of borrowed chords, as few as two or three as in Figures 7.8 and 7.9, or, at the other extreme, a series long enough to give the aural impression of a definite establishment of a minor key within a major framework, as in Figure 7.10.

Fig. 7.7.

Brahms, Symphony No. 2 in D Major, Op. 73

G: I   IV   I   IV   I   V⁷   i   V⁷   i

I   V⁷   i   V⁷   (i)   ♭VI

i   I

Fig. 7.8.

Rossini, *Messe Solennelle*, "Cum Sancto Spiritu"

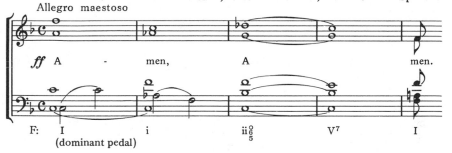

Allegro maestoso

ff   A   -   men,   A   men.

F: I   i   ii$^{\varnothing}_{\substack{6\\5}}$ V⁷   I

(dominant pedal)

Fig. 7.9.

Chorale Prelude, *O Mensch, bewein dein
Sünde gross* (*Orgelbüchlein*, No. 23)

Adagio assai

E♭:   i₆   I₆   ii₆   II₆   iii₆   III₆   IV₆   V$_{\substack{6\\5}}$ I   ♭VI   ii$^{\varnothing}_{6}$ ii°⁷   I$_{\substack{6\\4}}$ V   I

Fig. 7.10.

Mässig geschwind

Schubert, *Jägers Liebeslied,* Op. 96, No. 2

D: I   ♭VI ♭III   iv i   V i V I₆

Terminology Variant

In some systems of chord classification, the tonic center for a major key and its parallel minor represent a single tonality in which all chords, as found in either scale, are diatonic. Thus, for example, all the chords of C major and C minor are diatonic in the tonality of C; chords with the same roots are interchangeable, eliminating the necessity of designating any chord as an altered chord.

Assignment 7.2. Harmonic analysis. Copy out excerpts as assigned. Write in chord numbers below bass staff and identify non-harmonic tones.

Chopin: Mazurkas

   No. 1 (Op. 6, No. 1), measures 12–16
   No. 8 (Op. 7, No. 4), measures 1–4
   No. 20 (Op. 30, No. 3), measures 12–16

Mendelssohn, *Songs Without Words*

   No. 15 (Op. 38, No. 3), measures 11–5 from end
   No. 49 (Op. —) measures 8–4 from end

Mozart: Sonatas for Piano

   F Major, K. 533, first movement, measures 24–26
   C Major, K. 309, third movement, measures 143–149

APPLICATION

Written Materials

Part-Writing Rule 10. Use of altered chords does not change part-writing procedure. *Do not* double any altered note. Use Rule 6A if unusual doubling occurs. A lowered altered tone usually proceeds downwards; a raised altered tone proceeds upwards. *Exception:* the altered root of a major triad may be doubled; one of these roots is often resolved by leap.

Assignment 7.3. Fill in alto and tenor voices. Make harmonic analysis.

(3)

Assignment 7.4. Write a short original composition, making use of the chords studied in this chapter. The composition may be in four-voice chorale style, for piano solo, or for voice or solo instrument and piano.

Ear Training

Exercise 7.1. Sing the following progressions, using letter names in major keys indicated by the instructor.

I IV V I; I iv V I   I vi IV V I; I ♭VI iv V I
I ii V I; I ii° V I   I vii°⁷ I; I vii^{d7} I
I ii⁷ V I; I ii°⁷ V I   I IV vii°⁷ I; I iv vii^{d7} I
I V vi; I V ♭VI

Exercise 7.2. Harmonic dictation will now include examples of borrowed chords.

Keyboard Harmony

Exercise 7.3. Play chord progressions from Exercise 7.1 at the keyboard in any major key, as assigned. Use inversions where necessary (as in the ii° triad) or where desirable.

8

Secondary Dominant Chords

THEORY AND ANALYSIS[1]

All secondary dominant chords are major triads or major-minor seventh chords, so named because they often seem to have the effect, at least temporarily, of a dominant chord. This is especially true when the root of the following chord is a fifth below the root of the secondary dominant. Any major or minor triad may be given the temporary effect of a tonic by preceding it with a major triad or major-minor seventh chord in a dominant relationship to the temporary tonic.[2]

Fig. 8.1.

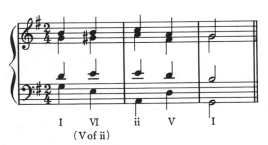

	I	VI	ii	V	I
		(V of ii)			

In Figure 8.1, the vi triad (E G B) has been altered to become a VI triad (E G♯ B). The progression VI-ii has a temporary effect of dominant and tonic; however, no further attempt is made to establish the key of A minor,

---

[1]Review *Elementary Harmony: Theory and Practice,* Chapter 20, which presents the study of one secondary dominant chord, the dominant of the dominant (II or V of V), as well as terminology variants for secondary dominant chords and the use of the dominant of the dominant in a transient modulation.

[2]Secondary leading tone chords, presented in Chapter 9, produce the same effect. These are diminished triads and diminished seventh chords built upon the "leading tone," a note a half step below the chord of resolution.

and the progression follows normally in G major. In the analysis of Figure 8.1, the VI chord is also designated V of ii, a symbol that identifies a chord whose root is a fifth above (fourth below) the root of the ii triad, and thus standing in dominant relationship to the ii triad. The same type of symbol may be used for any secondary dominant triad or seventh chord.

The secondary dominant chords may be classified in three groups:

GROUP I. *Altered chords that function as a secondary dominant to a diatonic triad in the key.* The chords of this group comprise the great majority of secondary dominant usages. Note that the I triad in a minor key is a secondary dominant only when used within the phrase; the "picardy third" at the cadence is not a secondary dominant.

Fig. 8.2.

Major keys

II	III	VI	VII	II⁷	III⁷	VI⁷	VII⁷	I⁻⁷
V of V	V of vi	V of ii	V of iii	V⁷of V	V⁷of vi	V⁷of ii	V⁷of iii	V⁷of IV

Minor keys

I	II	I⁷	II⁷
V of iv	V of V	V⁷of iv	V⁷ of V

GROUP II. *Unaltered chords that function as a secondary dominant to a diatonic triad in a key.* These occur only in a minor key. Of the chords in this group, III, VII, and VII⁷ function as secondary dominant chords while also serving their normal function as diatonic chords in the key. For the III⁷ to become a secondary dominant, its seventh must be lowered, III ⁷.

The IV triad has two functions also. One studied earlier is that as a substitute for the iv triad when an ascending melodic line passes through the sixth scale step, with the resulting progression IV-vii°₆ or IV₆-V₆. As a secondary dominant, IV and IV⁷ function as V of VII which can easily precede a series of diatonic "secondary dominant" triads: IV-VII-III-VI (V of VII- V of III-V of VI-VI).

Fig. 8.3.

III	IV	VII	III⁻⁷	IV⁷	VII⁷
V of VI	V of VII	V of III	V⁷ of VI	V⁷ of VII	V⁷ of III

GROUP III. *Altered or unaltered chords which are secondary dominants to other altered chords.* The use of the chords of this group range from infrequent to rare. The ♭III and ♭VI in major keys have already been considered as borrowed chords, and when used in succession, the first of these functions as a secondary dominant to the second, as shown in Figure 7.10. The use of ♭VI as a secondary dominant to ♭II or N_6 (Neapolitan sixth chord) will be considered in Chapter 10.

Should a composer choose on occasion to use a major or minor triad with any variety of alteration, no matter how unusual, this chord can be preceded by its secondary dominant. The ♯IV and ♯IV⁷ (V of vii, V⁷ of vii) are included in Figure 8.4 only as a representative of this possibility; the ♯IV⁷ is shown in actual usage in Figure 8.19, where in E major we find the progression A♯ C✕ E♯ G♯–D♯ F♯ A♯ (♯IV⁷-vii) as a part of a sequence of root movements by fifths.

Fig. 8.4.

Major keys   Minor keys

♭III   ♯IV   ♭VI   ♭III⁻⁷   ♯IV⁷   ♭VI⁻⁷   VI
V of ♭VI   V of vii   V of ♭II   V⁷of ♭VI   V⁷of vii   V⁷of ♭II   V of ♭II
(V of N₆)   (V⁷of N₆)   (V of N₆)

Assignment 8.1. Spell each secondary dominant triad and seventh chord as found in Figure 8.2 in any major or minor key.

Use of Individual Secondary Dominant Chords

a) Normal resolution. A single secondary dominant chord with its normal resolution may be found during the course of a phrase of music. The chords of Group I (Figure 8.2), as well as those designated as diatonic or borrowed chords from Groups II and III, are commonly used in this manner. The remaining secondary dominant chords are ordinarily found only in a series of secondary dominant chords or in a harmonic sequence, as will be discussed later in the chapter.

Figures 8.5 and 8.6 serve to illustrate the use of all secondary dominant chords used singly. The root of the secondary dominant progresses up by fourth (down by fifth) to the root of the following chord. In listening to each example, note the temporary but definite feeling of tonic created in the progression of the two chords. These are not considered modulations because no new key is established.

Fig. 8.5. VI, III, major key

Mussorgsky, *Khovantchina*, Act II

I └VI ii┘ V └III   vi┘   I

Fig. 8.6.

Mozart, Concerto in A Major for Piano
and Orchestra, K. 488

A: I III⁶₅ vi ii⁶ I⁶₄ V⁷ I
                        V⁶₅of vi

When a secondary dominant (or any other altered or dissonant harmony) is built above the tonic note, the sonority loses its function as a tonic chord. The major tonic triad in a minor key (except at the final cadence) and the major-minor seventh chord built upon the tonic in both major and minor keys function as secondary dominant to the subdominant harmony (V of IV).

The I⁻⁷ (V⁷of IV) is dramatically presented as the first chord of the opening movement of Beethoven's First Symphony. Its resolution strongly establishes a key feeling of F, which is promptly dissipated in the following measure. This in turn is followed by another secondary dominant progression II⁷-V (V⁷of V-V) strongly implying G major, which again proves not to be the key when hearing the final resolution of the phrase in C major.

Fig. 8.7.

Beethoven, Symphony No. 1, Op. 21

C: I⁻⁷   IV   V⁷   vi   II⁷   V
      V⁷of IV   V⁷of V

The V^7 of IV with normal resolution can also be seen in Figure 7.2, first chord of measure 2.

In Figure 8.8, the minor tonic triad is altered to become a major tonic triad with a function of V of iv, while Figure 8.9 shows the same chord function with an added seventh.

Fig. 8.8. I (V of iv)

Brahms, Intermezzo, Op. 116, No. 2

Fig. 8.9. I^7 (V^7 of iv)

Bach, *Well—tempered Clavier*, "Prelude XXII"

b) Succession of the altered and unaltered form of the chord. As with other altered chords, the immediate succession of two forms of the chord can be most effective. In the two examples from Brahms in Figure 8.10, we find the progressions ii°⁷-II⁷ and II⁷-ii°⁷ respectively.

Fig. 8.10.

Brahms, Intermezzo, Op. 118, No. 4

(a) Allegretto

Brahms, Intermezzo, Op. 117, No. 3

(b) Più lento

c) Interruption of a "normal" progression. In a "normal" progression, the second of the two triads may be preceded by its secondary dominant, as in the following illustration where VI (V of ii) interrupts the normal progression IV-ii.

Fig. 8.11.

Schubert, *Lob der Tränen*, Op. 13, No. 2

Lenz und Ju - gend - lust;

In an extension of this principle, the normal progression is interrupted by two successive secondary dominants. Figure 8.12 shows a basic progression I-IV-V-vi. In IV-V, V is preceded by its secondary dominant II (V of V) which in turn is preceded by its secondary dominant VI (V of V of V). The same pattern is repeated in the progression V-vi.

Fig. 8.12.

Johann Stamitz (1717—1757), Symphony, Op. 5, No. 2

The harmonic pattern can be represented as follows:

The progression of the secondary dominant to its temporary tonic may at times be preceded by a chord which would produce a normal progression in the key of the temporary tonic. Figure 8.13 contains the progression $\text{II}_6\text{-III}_6\text{-vi}$; the first two of these constitute neither a "normal" progression in the key of the phrase (G major) or a regular resolution of II^7 ($\text{V}^7\text{of V}$) by root movement down a fifth. The goal of these two altered chords is vi, but by considering vi as a temporary tonic, i, the progression proves to be $\text{IV}_6\text{-V}_6\text{-i}$ in the temporary key of E minor.

Fig. 8.13.

Bach, *Herr Jesu Christ, dich zu uns wend* (♯136)

d) The embellishing secondary dominant chord. An embellishing chord may be defined as one which appears between two chords, both of which have the same root. Secondary dominants are commonly used as embellishing chords, giving a temporary effect of I-V-I.

Fig. 8.14. V-II-V, minor key

Brahms, *Vom verwundeten Knaben,*
Op. 14, No. 2

Andantino

The embellishing secondary dominant chord may also be found less commonly between two chords with the same normal resolution, such as ii-Vofii-IV, or, even more rarely, between two occurrences of a chord that is not the resolution of the secondary dominant, as in Figure 8.15: ii-III-ii (ii-Vofvi-ii).

Fig. 8.15.   Brahms, *An die Nachtigall,*
                                                  Op. 46, No. 4

e) *Other resolutions of the secondary dominant.*   A commonly used progression in diatonic triads is the deceptive progression V-vi. A secondary dominant chord may also take advantage of this possibility. The most common example of this deceptive progression is III-IV (Vof vi-IV), which however turns out to be merely a chromatic form of the common progression iii-IV (Figure 8.16). For an example of II-iii (Vof V-iii), see Figure 3.17.

Fig. 8.16.

Haydn, Quartet in G Major, Op. 77, No. 1, first movement

Other resolutions of secondary dominant chords are less frequent. The progression $I^{-7}\text{-}VI^7$ (V^7 of IV-V^7 of ii) in the next illustration is made possible by the use of $\frac{4}{2}$ inversions in the chromatically descending bass line.

Fig. 8.17.

Franck, *Pièce Héroique*

Other secondary dominant chords can be approached in the same way; for example: ii-ii$_4$-VII or ii-II$_4$-VII, IV-IV$_4$-II or IV-IV$^{-7}_4$-II, V-V$_4$-III.

Secondary Dominant Chords in the
Harmonic Sequence

The effectiveness of the familiar and much-used device of harmonic sequence is greatly enhanced through the additional possibilities for variety when using altered chords, including both the borrowed chords and secondary dominant chords studied to this point.

The common cycle of root movements by fifth could be expressed by an uninterrupted series of secondary dominant chords: I-IV-VII-III-VI-II-V-I (I-Vof-Vof-Vof-Vof-Vof-V-I). Although a series of such length is rare, the excerpt from Beethoven, Figure 8.18, shows such a series altered only by the absence of IV and the interpolation of vi after VI.

Fig. 8.18.

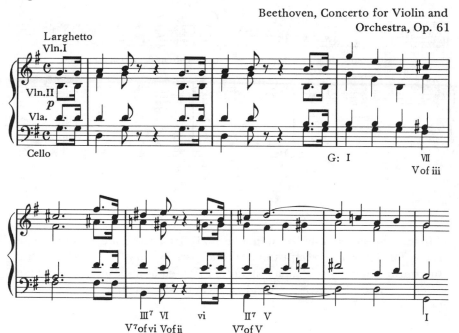

Beethoven, Concerto for Violin and
Orchestra, Op. 61

In Figure 8.19, Schumann gives the same series of root movements an entirely different character by alternating secondary dominants and diatonic triads, and by the use of the rare vii triad instead of vii° (in E major, D♯ F♯ A♯ instead of D♯ F♯ A) and preceded by its secondary dominant, the rarely used ♯IV⁷ (V⁷ofvii).

Fig. 8.19.

Schumann, *Liederkreis,* "Waldesgespräch,"
Op. 39, No. 3

In the sequence of fifths in a minor key, VII, III, and VI are diatonic major triads. The following excerpt from Handel uses the complete series of fifths (but substituting iv for ii°), and includes IV⁷ used as a secondary dominant (V⁷of VII) and the altered seventh added to III, creating the secondary dominant V⁷of VI.

Fig. 8.20.

Handel, *Messiah,* "How Beautiful Are the
Feet of Them"

The effectiveness of any harmonic sequence can be heightened by similar devices. Worth careful study are the three excerpts following from works of Bach, Beethoven, and Brahms, each using the basic progression I-vi-ii-vii°-iii (roots down a third, up a fourth) but with different selections for the quality of each chord.

Bach	I^{-7}	VI^7	II^7	VII^7	III^7
Beethoven	I	VI	ii	VII	iii
Brahms	I	vi	ii	vii°^{7}	III^7

Fig. 8.21.

Bach, *Brandenburg Concerto* No. 2[3]

(Allegro)

[3]This reduction from the score omits the several contrapuntal lines included in the orchestral texture. Each measure of the melody shown here in the treble clef is played by a different instrument in turn. In the full score, which should be examined, each chord is arpeggiated, allowing normal resolution of each chromatic tone instead of resolutions by leap implied in the block chords of this figure.

Fig. 8.22.

Beethoven, Sonata in E♭ Major for Piano,
Op. 81a, third movement

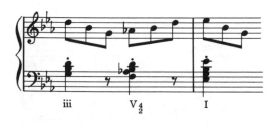

Fig. 8.23.

Brahms, *Von ewiger Liebe,* Op. 43, No. 1

Assignment 8.2. Harmonic analysis.   Copy out examples as assigned. Write in chord numbers below staff and identify non-harmonic tones.

Beethoven: Sonatas for Piano

No. 3 (Op. 2, No. 3), second movement, measures 1–8
No. 4 (Op. 7), second movement, measures 1–24[4]
No. 6 (Op. 10, No. 2), first movement, measures 1–12
No. 7 (Op. 10, No. 3), third movement, trio, measures 1–17
No. 10 (Op. 14, No. 2), second movement, measures 17–20

Chopin: Mazurkas

No. 4 (Op. 6, No. 4), measures 1–4
No. 11 (Op. 17, No. 2), measures 1–12
No. 21 (Op. 30, No. 4), measures 68–76
No. 24 (Op. 33, No. 3), measures 1–10
No. 26 (Op. 41, No. 1), measures 17–24

Mendelssohn: *Songs Without Words*

No. 1 (Op. 19, No. 1), measures 3–6
No. 13 (Op. 38, No. 1), measures 1–5

Mozart: Sonatas for Piano

G Major, K. 283, third movement, measures 73–81
B♭ Major, K. 281, third movement, measures 1–4
B♭ Major, K. 333, first movement, measures 46–50

Schumann: *Album for the Young,* Op. 68

No. 26, measures 1–4
No. 24, measures 1–8

Murphy and Melcher, *Music for Study,* Chapter 18

APPLICATION

Written Materials

In writing secondary dominant chords, follow Part-writing Rule 10. Procedures for the doubling and resolution of secondary dominant seventh chords are the same as for the dominant seventh (V^7) chord (review *Elementary*

---

[4]In measure 18, the chord over the bass note G♯ is ♯v^{d7} (see Chapter 9).

Harmony; Theory and Practice, Chapter 19). The treatment of the altered tone in these and other altered chords often needs special consideration, as follows:

a) In arpeggiated or otherwise florid arrangements of a chord, the resolution of the altered tone may seem to be unorthodox or may be delayed. *Example:* Figure 8.10*a*), measure 3, the B natural is assumed to resolve to middle C rather than to the lower C which immediately follows.

b) A tone chromatically raised may descend to a pitch one half step lower in the next chord provided that both notes of the half step interval use the same letter name. *Examples:* (1) Figure 8.10*b*), progression II⁷-ii°⁷ (V⁷of V-ii°⁷), half step interval F×-F♯, (2) Figure 8.18, progression VII-III⁷ (V of iii-V⁷of vi), half step interval A♯-A♮. Also, review *Elementary Harmony: Theory and Practice,* page 322 and Figure 20.14.

c) In a progression of a secondary dominant to its temporary tonic, the spelling of any non-harmonic tones during the progression is determined by the scale of the key of the temporary tonic. *Example:* Figure 8.19, measure 2, progression ♯IV⁷-vii (V⁷of vii-vii). The temporary tonic, represented by vii, is D♯ minor; therefore the vocal line includes the pitches B♯ and C×, the raised sixth and seventh scale steps of D♯ minor.[5]

d) When the root of a secondary dominant chord is an altered tone, it may, of course, move in any way normal to a usual V-I progression. This root may also be doubled. *Example:* Figure 8.19, ♯IV⁷ (V⁷of iii), the root, A♯ is doubled, and the root in the bass moves by fifth to the root of the following triad.

e) *The cross-relation.* When each of two chords in succession contains the same letter name, and one is chromatically altered, this pair of letter names is usually found in one voice line. In Figure 8.24*a*) there is a chromatic alteration A♭ to A♮ in the chord progression F A♭ C - F A C. This alteration should occur in a single voice line, as in this example, where the chromatic progression appears in the bass line.

Were the chromatic alteration found between two different voices, *cross-relation* (also known as *false-relation*) would result. In Figure 8.24*b*) we have rearranged the notes so that the A♭ in the bass is followed by an A♮ in the soprano. It is best to avoid cross-relations, especially in music with a constant number of voice lines. In the free voicing technique of keyboard style, the cross-relation can sometimes be used effectively, but its use should be restricted to those few places where other features of the composition detract from the prominence of the cross-relation. Two such features which are often used to soften the effect of a cross-relation are (1) a chord in $\frac{4}{2}$ inversion at the point of the second note of the cross-relation, as in Figure 8.25, and (2) the use of a diminished seventh chord at the same point (see Chapter 9).

---

[5] Review *Elementary Harmony: Theory and Practice,* pp. 321–322, for discussion of a similar treatment of the fifth of the II⁷ (V⁷of V) in minor keys.

Fig. 8.24.

Hymn: Maryton

cross-relation

Fig. 8.25.

Bach, Prelude in C Minor (organ)

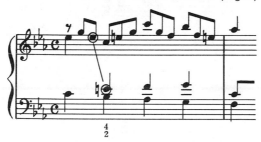

Assignment 8.3. Part-writing.   Fill in alto and tenor voices. Make harmonic analysis.

(1)

Assignment 8.4. *a)* Write, in four voices, chord progressions from Exercises 8.1 and 8.2 in keys as assigned. Use any appropriate inversions and non-harmonic tones. Also, devise other progressions using secondary dominant chords, borrowed chords, and triads not found in these exercises, as explained in Exercise 8.2.

b) Using these same chord progressions, write a short piece in piano style, as studied in Chapter 4. Figure 8.26 shows one possibility for realizing chord progression number 4 from Exercise 8.1.

Fig. 8.26.

PROJECT I (cont.). *Realization of figured basses.*
Assignment 8.5.

Handel, Sonata in A Major for Violin

Assignment 8.6. This is the second half of a binary form. The first half started in G minor and modulated to D minor.

Marcello, Sonata in G Minor for Flute or Violin

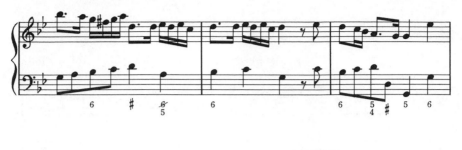

PROJECT II (cont.) *Harmonizing folksongs.*

Assignment 8.7. Melody harmonization.   Harmonize folk melodies, using examples of borrowed chords and secondary dominant chords. Write harmonization as vocal solo with piano accompaniment, and indicate tempo and dynamic markings. In a harmonization, altered chords should be used sparingly. It is better to have a few well-chosen altered chords which progress logically and smoothly to their following chords; excessive use of altered chords limits their effectiveness.

(1)   U.S. Folksong

mar - ry me If ev - er he mar -ried a - ny.

(2) Scotch Folksong

O, John my___ love come___ kiss me now, O,___

John my___ love come___ kiss me now,___ O, ___

John come_ kiss me___ by and by, For well you know the

way to woo. Oh! some will court_ and_ com - pli - ment, and

oth - er some_will___ kiss a - new, And___ some will hug___ in___

oth - er's arms and that's the___ way I like to do.

(3) English Folksong

With my flock as walk - ed I,___ the plains___ and mount - ains

o - ver, Late, a dam - sel pass'd me by;___

With an in - tent to move her, I stept in her way, she

stept a - way, But oh! I shall ev - er love her.

(4)   English Folksong

'Twas on a Mon - day morn - ing when I be - held my

dar - ling she looked so neat and charm - ing in

ev' - ry high de - gree._____ She looked so neat and

nim - ble O, a - wash - ing of her lin - en O,

dash-ing a - way with the smooth-ing iron, dash-ing a - way with the

smooth - ing iron, she stole my heart__ a - way._____

(5)   French Folksong

Oh God, Thy lit - tle Stran - ger is here to - day on

earth._____ A ho - ly trans - for - ma - tion, the mys - t'ry of His

birth._____ Thy word is so lof - ty, so might-y; a prom -ise from

God th'E -ter - nal One_____ Makes mort - al here to - day_____ The

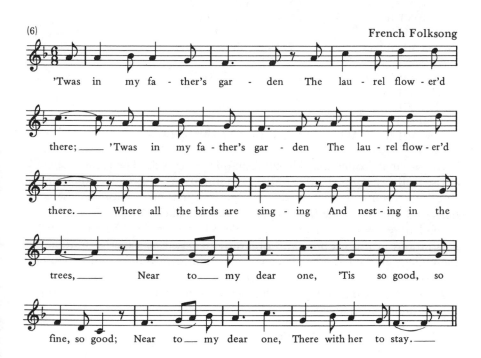

love of God on high,____ 'Tis giv'n to man be - low.____

(6)   French Folksong

'Twas in my fa - ther's gar - den The lau - rel flow - er'd

there;____ 'Twas in my fa - ther's gar - den The lau - rel flow - er'd

there.____ Where all the birds are sing - ing And nest - ing in the

trees,____ Near to__ my dear one, 'Tis so good, so

fine, so good; Near to__ my dear one, There with her to stay.____

PROJECT III (cont.). *Composing an original melody and accompaniment to a given text.*

Assignment 8.8. Using poems from Assignment 4.8, or a poem of your choice, continue work in Project III, making use of secondary dominant chords and borrowed chords as part of the harmonic texture.

PROJECTS IV AND V (cont.). *Composing original music.*

Assignment 8.9. Continue work in these projects, using secondary dominant chords and borrowed chords as part of the harmonic texture.

Ear Training

Exercise 8.1. Sing each of the following progressions, using letter names, in any major key indicated by the instructor. Repeat each exercise, adding a seventh to each secondary dominant chord.

1. I II V I	*or*	I VofV V I
2. I VI ii V I		I Vofii ii V I
3. I VI II V I		I Vofii VofV V I
4. I III vi ii V I		I Vofvi vi ii V I
5. I III vi II V I		I Vofvi vi VofV V I
6. I III VI II V I		I Vofvi Vofii VofV V I
7. I III IV V I		I Vofvi IV V I
8. I vi VII iii vi ii V I		I vi Vofiii iii vi ii V I
9. I vi VII iii VI ii V I		I vi Vofiii iii Vofii ii V I
10. I vi VII iii vi II V I		I vi Vofiii iii vi VofV V I
11. I vi VII III IV V I		I vi Vofiii Vofvi IV V I

There are many other possible combinations of chords. The student should devise further examples, using various combinations of secondary dominants (triads or seventh chords), unaltered chords (triads or seventh chords), and borrowed chords (triads and seventh chords). Such progressions may be normal progressions as defined in Table 3.1, progressions based on music illustrations in this chapter, and progressions based on experimentation by the student. In the last named, a secondary dominant is not usually followed by a borrowed chord, nor does the reverse occur.

Exercise 8.2.   Sing each of the following progressions, using letter names, in any minor key indicated by the instructor.

1. i II V i	*or*	i VofV V i
2. i I⁷ iv V i		i V⁷ofiv V i
3. i iv⁷ VII⁷ III VI⁷ II⁷ V i		i iv⁷ V⁷ofIII III VI⁷ V⁷ofV V i
4. i III⁻⁷ VI II V i		i V⁷ofVI VI VofV V i

Exercise 8.3. Harmonic dictation.   Dictation exercises will now include examples of the secondary dominant chords.

Self-Help in Harmonic Dictation

The following hymn tune excerpts contain examples of secondary dominant chords.

I^{-7} *(major)*, *I*, I^7 *(minor)*,
V^7*ofIV*, *Vofiv*, V^7*ofiv*

Need 1–4	M-265
Sanky 5–8	M-514

Holy Ghost 1–4	E-57
Steadfast	E-283

III, III⁷,
Vofvi, V⁷ofvi

Unser Herrscher 9–12	M-7
Lobe den Herren 18–21	M-55
Nun freut euch 9–12	M-84
Horsley 4–8	M-218
Ewing 4–8	M-303
Commandments 4–5	M-307
Darwall's 148th 11–14	M-483
Vetter 1–2	E-160
Doncaster, all	E-293

VI, VI⁷,
Vofii, V⁷ofii

Park Street	M-25
St. Elizabeth 1–4, 9–13	M-79
Canterbury 5–8	M-135
Shaddick 5–8	M-186
Haydn 13–16	M-258
Manoah 9–16	M-403
Noel 13–16	E-19

Two or more different secondary
dominant chords

Cambridge 5–8	M-24
Stuttgart 5–8	M-63
Canonbury 1–2, 5–7	M-195
Rest 5–10	M-235
Eucharistic Hymn, all	M-320
Cobb 7–8	E-134

Keyboard Harmony

Exercise 8.4.   Play at the keyboard the chord progressions found in Exercises 8.1 and 8.2, in keys indicated by the instructor.

Exercise 8.5.   Improvise at the keyboard chord progressions not found in Exercises 8.1 and 8.2. Read explanatory material in Exercise 8.1.

Exercise 8.6.   Play the following additional chord progressions.

1. I I$_4^{-7}$ VI^7 ii V I   (I V^{7}ofIV VI^7 ii V I)
   $_2$

2. I V V$_4$ III^7 vi ii V I   (I V V$_4$ V^{7}ofvi vi ii V I)
   $_2$ $_2$

3. i iv^7 VII^7 III^7 VI^7 II^7 (V^{7}ofV) V (Sing the first phrase of Cole Porter's

All the Things You Are as you play this progression.)

4. i V$_6$ v$_6$ vi^{o7} ii$_4^o$ V i$_6$ II^7 (V^{7}ofV) V i
                  $_3$

5. i V$_6$ i$_4$ II$_4$ (V$_4^o$ofV) vii$_4^{d7}$ I$_4$ (V$_4^o$ofiv) iv i$_6$ V i
      $_2$ $_3$ $_3$ $_3$ $_3$ $_3$ $_4$

Exercise 8.7. Melody harmonization at the keyboard.   Secondary dominants may be used in a harmonization when the melody note is part of a
secondary dominant chord and the melody note(s) following will allow a
logical resolution of the secondary dominant. For example, the second phrase
from melody number 24, *Music for Sight Singing*, may be harmonized as follows
(instead of I/I/I V/I):

Fig. 8.27.

The following melodies, all from *Music for Sight Singing*, may be harmonized
with secondary dominant chords, as indicated. (Review *Elementary Harmony:
Theory and Practice*, Chapter 20, for the II and II^7; VofV and V^{7}of V.)

VI or VI^7 (Vofii): 43, 139, 144
III or III^7 (Vofvi): 44, 81
I^{-7} (VofIV): 68, 116, 261, 370

The following additional melodies can be harmonized with secondary
dominants. The student should choose the appropriate chord: 32, 33, 109,
196, 327.

9

Secondary Leading Tone Chords;
Other Non-dominant
Diminished Seventh Chords

THEORY AND ANALYSIS

The study of chords with a dominant function have included, up to this point, the V (major) triad, the vii° (diminished) triad, and their sevenths, V^7, $vii°^7$, and vii^{d7}, all of which normally progress to the tonic triad. We have found that major triads and major-minor sevenths may also function as dominants to chords other than the tonic and that these are called secondary dominant chords. Now we shall see that diminished triads and their sevenths may function in relation to chords other than the tonic just as vii° does in relation to the tonic. These diminished triads or seventh chords are built upon a note a half step below the root of the following triad. The root of the diminished triad therefore acts as a leading tone to the root of the following chord, and for this reason these diminished triads and seventh chords are known as secondary leading tone chords.

In Figure 9.1*a*, the progression $vii°_6$-I or vii^{d7}-I represents a dominant relationship because of the root movement, leading tone to tonic, B-C. Similarly, in Figure 9.1*b*, the progression $\sharp iv°_6$-V or $\sharp iv^{d7}$-V represents a secondary dominant relationship because of the root movement of a leading tone, F$\sharp$, to the dominant, G (F$\sharp$-G). The $\sharp iv°$ or $\sharp iv^{d7}$ is a secondary leading tone chord to V.

Fig. 9.1.

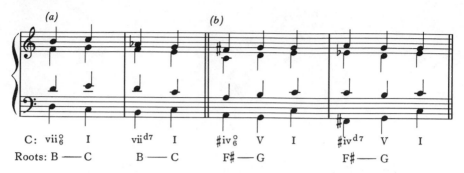

C: viiᵒ₆   I   vii^{d7}   I   ♯ivᵒ₆   V   I   ♯iv^{d7}   V   I

Roots: B —— C   B —— C   F♯ —— G   F♯ —— G

Figure 9.2 shows each of the possible secondary leading tone triads to major and minor triads in a key. Those marked with an * are infrequently used.

Fig. 9.2.

(a) Major keys

The ii° triad is, of course, a diatonic triad, but may be considered a secondary leading tone triad when its root resolves up a half step to the root of the III triad. The same may be said for vi° in relation to VII.

When adding a seventh to these triads, and using only notes diatonic in the key, the resulting seventh chord is sometimes a half diminished seventh chord and sometimes a fully diminished seventh chord. Those which are naturally half diminished may be made fully diminished seventh chords by chromatically lowering the seventh one half step, and it is in this form that the leading tone seventh is most commonly found. In fact, except for those above vii° and ♯iv°, half diminished leading tone seventh chords are infrequent in music.

Fig. 9.3.

(a) Major keys

(*b*) Minor keys

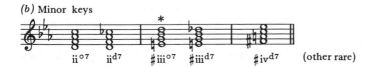

$$\text{ii}^{\circ 7} \qquad \text{ii}^{\text{d7}} \qquad \sharp\text{iii}^{\circ 7} \qquad \sharp\text{iii}^{\text{d7}} \qquad \sharp\text{iv}^{\text{d7}} \qquad \text{(other rare)}$$

Assignment 9.1. Spell secondary leading tone triads and seventh chords in each major and minor key, as shown in Figures 9.2 and 9.3. Concentrate on those indicated as commonly used (without an *).

Terminology Variants

These chords are often described and symbolized as incomplete forms of other chords. Diminished triads are considered to be incomplete dominant seventh chords with the root missing.[1] Thus $\sharp\text{i}^{\circ}$ is really VI^7 ($\text{V}^7\text{of ii}$) with its root missing: C$\sharp$ E G ($\sharp\text{i}^{\circ}$) = (A) C$\sharp$ E G (VI_7° or $\text{V}_7^{\circ}\text{of ii}$). Each diminished triad can therefore be shown to be one of the secondary dominant seventh chords with its root missing: $\sharp\text{ii}^{\circ}$ is an incomplete VII^7 (VII_7° or $\text{V}_7^{\circ}\text{of iii}$), $\sharp\text{iv}^{\circ}$ is an incomplete II^7 (II_7° or $\text{V}_7^{\circ}\text{of V}$), etc. The diatonic ii$^{\circ}$ triad in minor, when used as a secondary dominant, is an incomplete VII^7 (VII_7° or $\text{V}_7^{\circ}\text{of III}$).

The seventh chords in this system are considered to have the same missing root as the triad. Therefore, the complete chord would be a ninth chord (see Chapter 12). For example, in C major, the ninth chord D F$\sharp$ A C E$\flat$ (II^9 or $\text{V}^9\text{of V}$) with its root missing becomes F$\sharp$ A C E$\flat$ (II_9° or $\text{V}_9^{\circ}\text{of V}$), which, in Figure 9.3 is identified as $\sharp\text{iv}^{\text{d7}}$. In this variant, V_9° refers also to the half diminished seventh chord above $\sharp\text{iv}^{\circ}$, F$\sharp$ A C E. This same principle may be applied to all diminished seventh chords and half diminished seventh chords which function as secondary leading tone chords. (The placing of the subscript and superscript varies with different authorities: $\text{V}_{\circ}^9$, $_{\circ}\text{V}^9$, $^{\circ}\text{V}^9$ etc.)

These chords are also symbolized as "VIIof" or "VII^7of", or differentiated further by such symbols as $\text{VII}^{\circ 7}\text{of III}$, $\text{VII}^{\text{d7}}\text{of III}$, $\text{vii}^{\circ 7}\text{of iii}$, $\text{vii}^{\circ 7 \circ}\text{of iii}$, etc. Here is a partial list of symbols for the half diminished and fully diminished seventh chords built above F$\sharp$ in C major.

F$\sharp$ A C E	F$\sharp$ A C E$\flat$
$\sharp\text{iv}^{\circ 7}$	$\sharp\text{iv}^{\text{d7}}$
$\text{V}_{\circ}^9\text{of V}$	$\text{V}_9^{\circ}\text{of V}$
$\text{VII}^7\text{of V}$	$\text{VII}^7\text{of V}$
$\text{VII}^{\circ 7}\text{of V}$	$\text{VII}^{\text{d7}}\text{of V}$
$\text{vii}^{\circ 7}\text{of V}$	$\text{vii}^{\circ 7 \circ}\text{of V}$

---

[1]Review *Elementary Harmony: Theory and Practice,* pp. 191–192 and 218, for discussion of the concept that vii$^{\circ}$ is an incomplete V^7, symbolized V_7°.

As can be seen, some of these symbols are very complex; also, some pairs use the same symbol for both half diminished and fully diminished seventh chords. For these reasons, and for the sake of simplicity, only those symbols found in Figures 9.2 and 9.3 will be used in this text, though for those interested, there is no reason why these symbols cannot be translated into any of the symbols listed above.

Secondary Leading Tone Triads

Secondary leading tone triads, being diminished triads, are usually found in first inversion. The altered tone, found in an upper voice, functions as a leading tone and resolves upwards. Exceptions to this resolution are the same as for the altered tone of secondary dominant chords.

Fig. 9.4. #i°

Bach, *Gott lebet noch* (#234)

F: vi   IV   I₆   V⁴₃ I   V   #ii°₆   ii   I₆   V   I₆

Fig. 9.5. iii°

Bach, *Gottes Sohn ist kommen* (#18)

I   IV₆   iii°₆   IV   I

The iii°₆ of Figure 9.5 acts as an embellishing chord to IV.

In the next example (Figure 9.6), the #iv° is preceded by the secondary dominant chord III (V of vi). Were the triads of this progression diatonic, the progression would be normal, iii-IV-V⁷. In its altered form, III-#iv°-V⁷, it may still be considered a normal progression. Note the descending resolution of the secondary leading tone A# to A♮; the principle here is the same as for the altered tone in a secondary dominant chord.

Fig. 9.6. ♯iv°, major key

Beethoven, Quartet No. 8 in E minor, Op. 59, No. 2, second movement

E: I⁻⁷   IV   V⁷   III₆   ♯iv°₆   V⁷   I
V⁷of IV   V of vi

In Figure 9.7, the two secondary leading tone triads function as embellishing chords. Written in piano keyboard style, the secondary leading tones E♯ and A♯ may be considered as resolving up to one of the doubled roots F♯ and B respectively.

Fig. 9.7. ♯v°, ♯i°

Schumann, *Album for the Young*, Op. 68, No. 43

A: vi ♯v°₆ vi₆   ii ♯i°₆ ii₆

Secondary leading tone triads in a minor key are infrequently used. The ii° triad used as a secondary leading tone triad in Figure 9.8 appears on the weak part of the beat. This is an ambiguous use at best; the second beat might be analyzed in one of four ways: (1) F A♭ C E♭ is iv⁷ followed by passing tones, (2) iv⁷-ii°₆-III or (3) ii⁷of III-V°₇of III-III (review a similar situation in Figure 8.13), and (4) as in the example.

Fig. 9.8. ii°

Bach, *So wahr ich lebe, spricht dein Gott* (♯110)

c: i   v   ii°₆   III   V⁷   VI   V   i

In the next example, note the decorated downward resolution of the secondary leading tone, D♯-E-D♮.

Fig. 9.9. ♯iv°, minor key

Andante   Bach, *English Suite II,* "Sarabande"

♯iv⁰₆

Secondary Leading Tone Seventh Chords

Diminished seventh chords and half diminished seventh chords, unlike diminished triads, may be freely used in any inversion as well as with root in bass. The four notes of the fully diminished seventh chord equally divide the octave, making it impossible when hearing a single diminished seventh chord to determine its structure, that is, which note is root, third, fifth, or seventh. A diminished seventh chord and each of its inversions (Figure 9.10a) sounds the same as four successive diminished seventh chords, each with root in bass (Figure 9.10b).

Fig. 9.10.

(a)   (b)

It would appear from this that the spelling of a diminished seventh chord might be only a minor consideration. However, composers usually have been most careful in the spelling of the diminished seventh chord so that its leading tone function is clear in no matter what position the chord is found.

Figures 9.11 and 9.12 illustrate several diminished seventh chords in major keys: ♯i^d7, iii^d7, and ♯iv^d7, as well as vii^d7 previously studied. All are in root position with the movement of the root up a half step to the root of the following chord and the seventh down a half step.

Fig. 9.11.   **Schumann, Concerto in A Minor for Piano**
and Orchestra, op, 54

Fig. 9.12.

The $\sharp v^{d7}$ in root position with its normal resolution to vi can be seen in measure 2 of Figure 9.19 and measure 3 of Figure 9.26.

Half diminished seventh chords function in exactly the same way as the fully diminished seventh chords, as the $\sharp iv^{\circ 7}$ of the next example indicates.

Fig. 9.13. $\sharp iv^{\circ 7}$, major key

Wagner, *Die Meistersinger*, Act I

The diminished seventh chord in a minor key functions the same as in major. There is no ♯i^{d7} in minor since it would resolve to a diminished triad, ii°. Instead, ♯iii^{d7}, the first inversion of the theoretical ♯i^{d7}, resolves to iv. Figure 9.14 shows this and the ♯iv^{d7}. The ♯iii^{d7} has one voice missing because of the three-voice texture of the context in which it is found.

Fig. 9.14. ♯iii^{d7}, minor key   **Mozart, Sonata in F Major for Piano, K. 280, second movement**

Other secondary leading tone seventh chords in minor are uncommon.

When found in inversion, there is no change of spelling in these diminished seventh chords, even though to the ear the lowest sounding note could be the root of the chord. The actual root and seventh resolve exactly as in the root position of the chord.

Fig. 9.15.   **Brahms, Intermezzo, Op. 76, No. 7**

Resolution of ♯iv^d7 to Tonic Six-four

The ♯iv^d7 in both major and minor regularly resolves to the tonic six-four chord, as shown in Figure 9.16a and b.

Fig. 9.16.

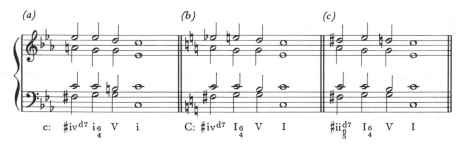

In both cases the root resolves up one half step, but to the fifth of the tonic chord. If one considers the sixth and fourth above the bass notes as non-harmonic tones resolving to the fifth and third, respectively, above the bass, then the progression may be identified as ♯iv^d7-V, a typical secondary leading tone chord usage.

Fig. 9.17. ♯iv^d7-i_6/4

Mozart, Sonata in G Major for Violin and Piano, K. 379, first movement

$I\,^6_4$

Fig. 9.18. ♯iv^{d7}-I^6_4

Allegro con brio

Beethoven, Concerto for Piano, No. 1, Op. 15,
first movement

cadenza

♯iv^{d7}   I^6_4

It will be observed in both Figures 9.16*b* and 9.18 (major keys) that the seventh of the ♯iv^{d7} is a chromatically lowered tone which ascends in its resolution (see also Figure 9.19, measure 4). To provide a chromatically raised note at this point, some composers at times spell the seventh of the ♯iv^{d7} in major keys enharmonically. In Figure 9.16*c*, the seventh E♭ is respelled as D♯, resulting in a ♯ii^{d7}, D♯ F♯ A C. Now we have a root, D♯, which ascends, but to the third of the I^6_4, and a seventh, C, which descends after having been held over into the I^6_4 chord. An example from literature can be seen in Figure 8.16, measure 2. In D major, the ♯ii^{d7}, E♯ G♯ B D, is the enharmonic spelling of the ♯iv^{d7}, G♯ B D F, allowing the resolution E♯-F♯ instead of F♮-F♯.

The Diminished Seventh Chord in a Harmonic Sequence

As with chords previously studied, diminished seventh chords can be used effectively in the harmonic sequence. Examples can be seen in Figures 9.11,

9.12, and 9.15*b*. In the latter, successive diminished seventh chords resolve to successive second inversions of triads, a use of second inversion not ordinarily encountered. Diminished chords not ordinarily encountered elsewhere may occasionally be found in a sequential passage, as the half diminished iii°⁷ of Figure 9.19.

Fig. 9.19.

Mozart, String Quartet, K. 458

The Non-dominant Use of Diminished Seventh Chords

There are two other diminished seventh chords commonly used in music that do not function as secondary leading tone chords. They are the ♯ii^{d7} and ♯vi^{d7} in major keys. In each of these, the root of the chord resolves up a half step to the third of the following chord[2]: ♯ii^{d7}-I₆ and ♯vi^{d7}-V₆ (or V₆/₅).

These chords are the enharmonic spellings of ♯iv^{d7} and ♯i^{d7} respectively, but, of course, function entirely differently from these leading tone chords.

Fig. 9.20.

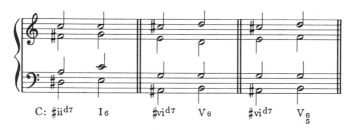

Figure 9.21 includes both chords, the ♯vi^{d7} being in inversion. When used in inversion, the roots of these chords still resolve up one half step to the third of the following chord. The ♯vi^{d7} with root in bass is seen in Figure 9.22.

---

[2]When ♯ii^{d7} is used in first inversion, it becomes the substitute for ♯iv^{d7} in the resolution to the tonic six-four chord, as explained on page 168.

Fig. 9.21.   **Beethoven, Quartet in D Major, Op. 18, No. 3,**
second movement

Fig. 9.22.   **Schumann,** *Dichterliebe,* **"Ich grolle nicht,"**
Op. 48, No. 7

Assignment 9.2.   Spell in each major key the ♯ii^{d7} and ♯vi^{d7} chords.

"Premature" Resolution of the Seventh

The seventh of any leading tone or secondary leading tone seventh chord is sometimes resolved normally before the resolution of the chord as a whole. This "premature" resolution produces a major-minor seventh chord that ordinarily resolves normally by root movement of a fifth.

Fig. 9.23.

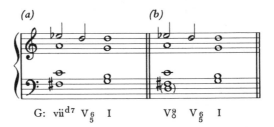

By applying the "missing root" concept, as in Figure 9.23*b*, the moving note appears to be a normal resolution, 9-8, over the root of the chord.[3]

---

[3]Study of ninth chords, including characteristics of their resolution, will be found in Chapter 12.

There is no single way to analyze the harmonic movement in this situation. In a slow harmonic movement, as in Figure 9.24, two distinct chords may be noted. In a more rapid harmonic movement, as in Figure 9.25, either of the two notes might be analyzed as a non-harmonic tone.

Fig. 9.24.   Berlioz, *La Damnation de Faust,* Part II, Scene 12

Fig. 9.25.   Bach, *Jesu, Meine Freude* (#356)

In Figure 9.26, the premature resolution of the seventh of $\sharp\text{iv}^{d7}$ produces a II_6 ($\text{V}_6\text{of V}$); these two chords together constitute an embellishing secondary dominant of V. See also Figure 9.19 in which the seventh of $\text{iii}^{\circ7}$ (I_9°) resolves prematurely to form a I^{-7} ($\text{V}^7\text{of IV}$).

Fig. 9.26.[4]   Mozart, Quintet for Clarinet and Strings, K. 581, second movement

[4]The part for clarinet in A has been transposed to concert pitch.

Irregular Resolutions

Resolution of secondary leading tone chords other than described in this chapter are uncommon, except in these situations:

1. When occurring over a note in a chromatic bass line. As previously described, the chromatic bass line will accommodate any series of chords and any resolutions. In Figure 9.27, bass line C-B-B♭-A, a diminished seventh chord appears over the note B; neither the chord nor the secondary leading tone, B, carries a normal resolution.

Fig. 9.27.

Wagner, *Lohengrin,* **Act III**

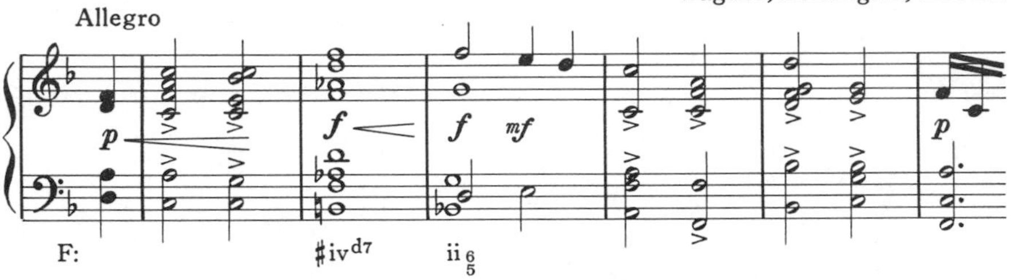

2. When the root of a secondary leading tone chord resolves up a half step but to a note other than the root of a chord. In Figure 8.8, measure 2, the root of D♯ F♯ A C resolves up a half step to the E of C E G (♯iv^d7-III₆). Observe, however, that the C E G triad only temporarily delays the normal resolution to E G♯ B.

3, When diminished seventh chords are found in succession. These chords may be used freely in succession and without concern for resolution of altered tones. The succession may produce a normal series of chords, as in Figure 9.28, or may produce an irregular series, such as the ♯iv-♯iii-vii-♯iv progression of Figure 9.29 (see also Figure 9.19, measures 3–4). When used as in the latter example, the series effectively obscures any feeling of key center until the resolution of the last chord of the series, which is ordinarily a normal resolution.

Fig. 9.28.

Berlioz, *Les Troyens à Carthage,* **Act I**

Fig. 9.29.

Bizet, *Les Pêcheurs des Perles,* Act II

Spelling Variants

Other than the substitution of ♯ii^d7 for ♯iv^d7 before the tonic six-four chord, spellings of diminished seventh chords other than those already indicated are infrequent. Composers may, at times, spell a diminished seventh chord contrary to its function, usually to facilitate reading. In Figure 9.30, the ♯iii^d7 in F♯ minor is spelled F𝄪 A♯ C♯ E♯ for two beats, and then changed to its correct spelling A♯ C♯ E G before resolving to IV. In this instance, the incorrect spelling would seem to be the more difficult of the two.

Fig. 9.30.

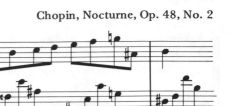

The Melodic Augmented Second

When using diminished seventh chords, the melodic interval of the augmented second sometimes appears. When the chord is arpeggiated, the interval from the seventh up to the root is an augmented second. The same is true when the chord is repeated in different positions (Figure 9.29, measures 3, 4, and 6).

Composers occasionally use this interval other than in a diminished seventh chord. In a minor key, a scale passage displayed prominently in the musical texture may include all or part of the harmonic form of the scale, ascending or descending.

Fig. 9.31.

The interval is also used as an appoggiatura figure where the second note of the augmented second is the dissonant tone (Figure 9.32, measure 1, E-F$^{\times}$). Although the interval is spelled as a second, it is large enough to be considered a leap in this context.

Fig. 9.32.

Mozart, Serenade No. 7, K. 250

Assignment 9.3. Harmonic analysis. Copy out excerpts as assigned. Write in chord numbers below staff and identify non-harmonic tones.

Bach: *371 Chorales*

No. 200, first phrase (♯iv°), No. 322, fourth phrase (♯i^{d7}), No. 138, sixth phrase, No. 113, fourth phrase (♯iii^{d7}), No. 24, second phrase, No. 167, fourth phrase (♯iv^{d7}), No. 67, sixth phrase (♯iv°^{7}), No. 24, second phrase (♯v^{d7}).

Beethoven: Sonatas for Piano

No. 1 (Op. 2, No. 1), first movement, measures 41–48; second movement, measures 45–46

No. 10 (Op. 14, No. 2), second movement, measures 1–16

No. 16 (Op. 31, No. 1), third movement, measures 55–60

Mendelssohn: *Songs Without Words*

No. 7 (Op. 30, No. 1), measures 28–30

No. 21 (Op. 53, No. 3), measures 1–8

No. 26 (Op. 62, No. 2), measures 41–47

Mozart: Sonatas for Piano

B♭ Major, K. 281, second movement, measures 36–43

C Major, K. 309, first movement, measures 14–8 from end; second movement, measures 11–8 from end

Schumann: *Album for the Young,* Op. 68

No. 13, measures 16–20

No. 16, last four measures

No. 28, last four measures

No. 32, measures 21–24

No. 41, measures 7–8

APPLICATION

Written Materials

The secondary leading tone triads and seventh chords, like secondary dominant chords, produce a temporary feeling of tonic on the following chord. Therefore, they are written as though they were vii$_6^\circ$-I or vii^{d7} (vii$^{\circ 7}$)-I progressions in the key of the chord that follows, implying these procedures:

 a) the root of the chord (the secondary leading tone) will ascend stepwise.

 b) the seventh in seventh chords will descend stepwise.

 c) any other altered tone will proceed as though in the key of the temporary tonic. For example, F minor, ♯iv^{d7}, B D F A♭: D is a raised sixth scale step in F minor, but is a diatonic second scale step in the key of the temporary tonic, C, and therefore may descend. See Figure 9.14. Of the regularly used secondary leading tone chords, ♯iv$^\circ$ and ♯iv^{d7} in minor are the only ones containing such an altered note.

 d) non-harmonic tones occurring during the secondary leading tone chord progression will be spelled in the key of the temporary tonic. These, however, are uncommon.

Additional helps in the part-writing of these chords are:

 e) the root of the secondary leading tone chord may descend a half step when using the same letter name, as in Figure 9.6, measure 3, alto A♯-A♮ in progressing from ♯iv$_6^\circ$ to V^7 in E major. A similar progression in Figure 9.9 contains an upper neighbor between the two notes in question (D♯-E-D♮).

 f) when diminished seventh chords are used in succession, altered tones may progress in any direction. See Figures 9.28 and 9.29.

 g) any cross relation between a note in a diminished seventh chord and a note in the preceding or following chord is acceptable. The strong characteristic sound of the diminished seventh chord detracts the ear from the usual unpleasant effect of the cross relation.

 h) unusual melodic intervals occur at times when using diminished seventh chords. When this chord is arpeggiated or repeated in a different soprano position, the melodic interval of the augmented second will often be found, as in Figure 9.29, measure 3. The root (secondary leading tone) of these chords is often approached by intervals such as the diminished fourth, the diminished fifth, or the diminished seventh. Observe the leap of the diminished fourth in going to ♯iv$_6^\circ$ in Figure 9.6, and in Bach chorale 365, measure 8, the leap of a diminished seventh in the bass. These leaps, always downwards, are followed by a change of direction in keeping with the principles of good melodic writing.

i) resolution of ♯iv°⁷. In resolving this half diminished seventh chord, care must be taken to avoid parallel fifths. The problem is identical to that encountered in the progression IV⁷-V (review pages 103–104). In Figure 9.13, fifths are avoided by use of a double suspension.

Assignment 9.4. Part-writing secondary leading tone triads.   Fill in alto and tenor voices. Write in harmonic analysis.

Assignment 9.5. Part-writing secondary leading tone seventh chords.   Fill in alto and tenor voices. Make harmonic analysis.

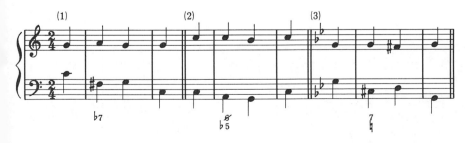

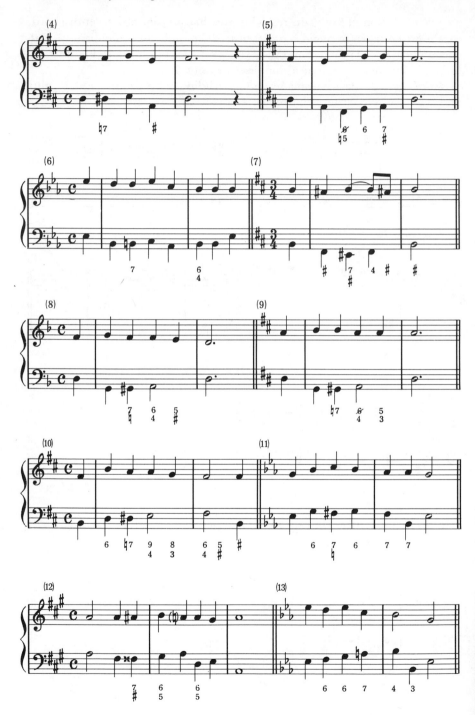

Assignment 9.6. Part-writing extended exercises including all secondary leading tone chords.

Assignment 9.7. Part-write chord progressions listed in Exercise 9.5 Choose key and meter. Add non-harmonic tones where feasible.

Assignment 9.8. Realize in keyboard style chord progressions from Exercises 9.1 and 9.5 (review Assignment 8.4*b*).

Assignment 9.9. Melody harmonization. The following phrases are from Bach chorales. In each, Bach has used a diminished seventh chord as studied in this chapter. Harmonize melodies as assigned, adding alto, tenor, and bass voices. Upon completion, compare your harmonization with that of Bach.

Sources: 1, chorale 47, last phrase; 2, chorale 67, last phrase; 3, chorale 94, last phrase; 4, chorale 128, fourth phrase; 5, chorale 237, last phrase; 6, chorale 303, fourth phrase; 7, chorale 340, fourth phrase.

Assignment 9.10. Melody harmonization. The following phrases are from songs by Robert Schumann. Harmonize each with a piano accompaniment. Compare your solution with the original. (Sources may be found in the first volume of Schumann songs in either the C. F. Peters or G. Schirmer edition.)

a) *Myrten*, "Was will die einsame Trane," Op. 25, No. 21, meas. 14–17.
b) Same as *a*), above, meas. 30–33.
c) *Frauen-Liebe und Leben*, "Ich kann's nicht fassen," Op. 42, No. 3, meas. 1–15.
d) *Frauen-Liebe und Leben*, "Du Ring an meinem Finger," Op. 42, No. 4, melody of piano postlude.
e) *Volksliedchen*, Op. 51, No. 2, meas. 29–33.

(a)   (Slowly)

(half cadence)

(b)   (Slowly)

(c)   (Rather fast)

(d)   (Moderate)

(e)   (Moderate)

PROJECTS I–V. Project assignments in Chapter 10 will include materials from this chapter.

Ear Training

Exercise 9.1.   Sing these progressions with letter names in any key indicated by the instructor.

1. I ♯iv° V I
2. I ♯iv^{d7} V I
3. I ♯iv°^{7} V I
4. I ♯i° ii V I
5. I ♯i^{d7} ii V I
6. I vi iii^{d7} IV V I

  7. I vi $\sharp$ii^{d7} iii IV V I
  8. I V $\sharp$v° vi ii V I
  9. I V $\sharp$v^{d7} vi IV V I
10. i $\sharp$iv° V i
11. i $\sharp$iv^{d7} V i
12. i $\sharp$iii^{d7} iv V i

Harmonic Listening

Identifying a diminished triad or diminished seventh chord by ear is easiest done by first identifying the chord of resolution. The diminished triad or seventh chord will have as its root a note a half step lower (one number lower and one letter name lower) than the chord of resolution. For example, if you identify a sonority as a diminished seventh chord, and the following chord is vi, the diminished seventh chord will be $\sharp$v^{d7}. But keep in mind the two exceptions, the non-dominant diminished seventh chords $\sharp$ii^{d7} and $\sharp$vi^{d7}. When the diminished seventh chord contains a note a *half step below the third* of the tonic triad, it is $\sharp$ii^{d7}; when the diminished seventh chord contains a note a *half step below the third* of the third of the dominant chord, it is a $\sharp$vi^{d7}. In the progression of a diminished seventh chord to tonic six-four, there is no way to tell by ear whether the chord is $\sharp$ii^{d7} or $\sharp$iv^{d7}.

When the resolution is irregular, that is, when the root of the chord of resolution is not preceded by its leading tone, it can be assumed that the composer probably spelled the chord with the bass note as its root. For example, if you heard the progression of Figure 9.27, you would not hear a leading tone (F$\sharp$) progressing to the root (G) of the ii$_{6}$ chord. Therefore, the bass note (B) of the diminished seventh chord is assumed to be the root of a $\sharp$iv^{d7}.

Many students find it helpful in listening to take advantage of the fact that there are only three possible diminished seventh chord sounds (not spellings). If, for example, we build diminished seventh chords on B, C, and C$\sharp$, the sound of any other diminished seventh chord will be that of an inversion of one of these three. This fact implies that every diminished seventh chord must contain one of these notes: the leading tone, the tonic, and the raised tonic, or its enharmonic equivalent, the lowered supertonic. If one of these tones can be heard, then the *most frequently used* diminished seventh chords can be identified as follows:

Note heard	*Major key*	*Minor key*
leading tone	vii^{d7}-I or $\sharp$v^{d7}-vi	vii^{d7}-i

Note heard	Major key	Minor key
tonic	$\sharp iv^{d7}$-I or $\sharp ii^{d7}$-I$_6$	$\sharp iv^{d7}$-i
raised tonic	$\sharp i^{d7}$-ii or $\sharp vi^{d7}$-V$_6$	
lowered supertonic		$\sharp iii^{d7}$-iv

This table will also aid in identifying diminished chords in succession and diminished seventh chords with irregular resolutions. If you can hear one of the three tones indicated, you will at least be able to identify the complete sound of the chord and to spell it satisfactorily, even if this is not the same as in the printed score. Referring again to Figure 9.27, the diminished seventh chord contains the tonic note, and in identifying the chord aurally, it can be labelled $\sharp iv^{d7}$. In a succession of diminished seventh chords, apply the same principle. In Figure 9.29, the four successive diminished seventh chords contain respectively the notes tonic, lowered supertonic, leading tone, and tonic. These can then be identified respectively as $\sharp iv^{d7}$, $\sharp iii^{d7}$, vii^{d7}, and $\sharp iv^{d7}$. In this instance, these are the actual spellings used by the composer.

Exercise 9.2. Harmonic dictation.   Harmonic dictation exercises will now include examples of the secondary leading tone triads and seventh chords.

Self-Help in Harmonic Dictation

St. Anthony's Chorale 1–5	M-6
Germany, all	M-36
Schumann, all	M-181
Perfect Love 13–16	M-333
Wie schön leuchtet 15–18	M-399
Stewart 9–16	E-46
McKee 5–8	E-263
Seymour 5–8	E-177
Nova Vita 7–13	E-375

Keyboard Harmony

Exercise 9.3.   Play Assignments 9.4 and 9.5 at the keyboard.

Exercise 9.4.   Play chord progressions from Exercise 9.1 at the keyboard, in any key as directed.

Exercise 9.5.   Play the following additional progressions in any major or minor key.

1. I ♯iv^{d7} V$^4_2$ I$_6$ vii$^{\circ}_6$ I

2. I ♯iv^{d7} vii^{d7}$^4_3$ I$_6$ vii$^{\circ}_6$ I

3. I ii ♯ii^{d7} I$_6$ ii$_6$ I$^6_4$ V I

4. I vi ♯vi^{d7} V$^6_5$ I ♯iv^{d7}$^6_5$ V^7 I

5. I ♯vi^{d7}$^6_5$ V$^4_3$ ♯ii^{d7} iii I$_6$ ♯v^{d7}$^4_3$ vi$_6$ ♯i^{d7} ii V I

6. I ♯iv^{d7} II$^6_5$ V ♯i^{d7}$^6_5$ VI$_4$ ii$_6$ vii^{d7}$^6_3$ V$_4$ I$_6$ ♯iv^{d7} I$^6_4$ V I

7. i ♯iii^{d7}$^6_5$ iv$_6$ ♯iv^{d7}$^6_5$ V i$_6$ vii^{d7}$^4_3$ ♯iv^{d7} V i

8. i i$_6$ ♯iii^{d7} I$^6_5$ iv ♯iv^{d7} II$^6_5$ V i

10

Augmented Triads
and the Neapolitan Sixth Chord

THEORY AND ANALYSIS

The Augmented Triad

An augmented triad is composed of two major thirds; the resulting distance from root to fifth of the triad is an augmented fifth, the inversion of which is the diminished fourth.

Fig. 10.1.

Assignment 10.1. Spelling the augmented triad.

a) Spell an augmented triad when any pitch name is given as the root. An augmented triad cannot be spelled from a root whose pitch name includes a double sharp. The fifth of the triad would then be a triple sharp.

b) Spell an augmented triad when any pitch name is given as the third.

c) Spell an augmented triad when the pitch name is the fifth.

Assignment 10.2. Intervals. a) Spell the interval of an augmented fifth from any given note (except a note with a double sharp).

b) Spell the interval of a diminished fourth from any given note.

The Augmented Triad in a Key

In a major key, all augmented triads are altered chords, the fifth of the triad being raised in each case. The most commonly used augmented triads in major are I+, IV+, and V+ (Figure 10.2a). In a minor key, only the III+ (Figure 10.2b) is regularly encountered. Its fifth is the leading tone of the key. All of these triads are used freely with root in bass or in first inversion; examples in second inversion are rare.

Fig. 10.2.

Assignment 10.3. Spell the I+, IV+, and V+ in each major key. Spell the III+ in each minor key.

In a major key, the altered tone is most commonly approached and left as a non-harmonic tone figure, usually passing tone or lower neighbor. The duration of the passing altered tone may be so brief as to make questionable an analysis of the sonority as an augmented triad, as in Figure 10.3 (Ab-A♮-B♭),

Fig. 10.3. I+

or the duration may be sufficiently long to make positive identification as a chord possible, as in the two examples from Figure 10.4 (E-E♯-F♯ and A-A♯-B).

Fig. 10.4. I+, IV+

Bizet, *Carmen*, Act I

The approach as a neighbor tone is common when the augmented triad is preceded and followed by a different chord, as in Figure 10.5 (E♯-D×-E♯ in I-V+-I).

Fig. 10.5. V+   Dvořák, Concerto for Violin in A Minor, Op. 53

Resolution of the augmented triad is determined by the necessity of re-solving the altered tone. Therefore, the usual progressions from the augmented triad are I+-IV (Figures 10.3 and 10.4), I+-ii$_6$, IV+-ii$_6$ (Figure 10.4), and V+-I (Figure 10.5).

In minor, the leading tone of the III+ triad is usually approached stepwise and resolved in the same ways as it would be under any other circumstances. In the progressions of the following two figures, note particularly the treatment of the leading tone.

Fig. 10.6. III+-VI   Bach, *Wir Christenleut* (#321)

g: II   III$_\substack{+ \\ 6}$ VI   IV$_6$ VII   V$_6$ i

Fig. 10.7. III+-#iv^{d7} Bach, *O Ewigkeit, du Donnerwort* (#26)

g: ii$^{\circ\substack{4 \\ 3}}$ III$_\substack{+ \\ 6}$ #iv^{d7}

There are other vertical sonorities which can be spelled as augmented triads, yet can be analyzed easily and equally well as major or minor triads containing a non-harmonic tone. In Figure 10.8, the root of the vi triad descends a half step in a passing tone figure, causing an augmented sonority with a chromatically lowered root.

Fig. 10.8.   Grieg, *Letzter Frühling*, Op. 34, No. 2

Andante

G: vi   (♭VI+)   I$_\substack{6 \\ 4}$ V^7 I

The sound of the first chord of measure 2 in Figure 10.9 is clearly augmented, yet appears to be simply a suspension in the V triad.[1]

Fig. 10.9.

Chopin, Nocturne, Op. 15, No. 3

The excerpt from the Schumann Concerto, Figure 10.10, appears to show a $III+_6^4$ and a $VI+_6^4$ preceding VI_6 and $\flat II_6$ (N_6)[2] respectively. The short duration of these augmented sonorities suggest that the third and fifth of each are simply appoggiaturas to the triads which follow.

Fig. 10.10.

Schumann, Concerto in A Minor for Piano and
Orchestra, Op. 54

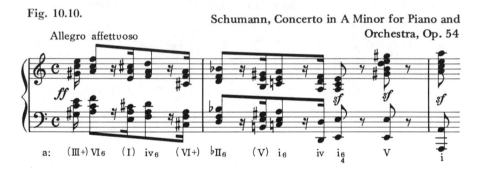

Again, and as demonstrated many times in similar situations in earlier chapters, the importance in analysis lies not in the identification of a sonority with an indisputable symbol, but in the understanding of the function of the sound in the musical context.

The Neapolitan Sixth Chord ($\flat II_6$)

The major triad built on the lowered second scale degree in either a major or minor mode is the $\flat II$. It is most often found in first inversion, hence the term sixth; there is no explanation for the term Neapolitan, but the chord

---

[1] Review *Elementary Harmony: Theory and Practice,* page 236, for the first presentation of this mediant sonority at the cadence.

[2] $\flat II_6$ and N_6 are described in following paragraphs.

is commonly known by this name. This chord is sometimes assigned the symbol "N$_6$".

Fig. 10.11.

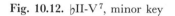

C: ♭II   ♭II$_6$(N$_6$)   c: ♭II   ♭II$_6$(N$_6$)

Assignment 10.4.   Spell the Neapolitan sixth chord in any major or minor key.

The Neapolitan sixth chord functions exactly as the diatonic ii$_6$ in major or ii$_6^\circ$ in minor, progressing either to tonic six-four or to the dominant. The progression ♭II$_6$-V always includes a melodic interval of the diminished third, lowered second scale degree to leading tone, as in Figure 10.12, measures 5–6, D♭-B.

Fig. 10.12. ♭II-V^7, minor key

Weber, *Der Freischütz*, Act I

Fig. 10.13. ♭II-I$_4^6$

Schubert, Quintet in C Major, Op. 163, first movement

The less common resolutions of the $\flat II_6$ in each of the following two examples can be explained in terms of the chromatic bass lines in each case.

Fig. 10.14. $\flat II$-$\sharp iv^{d7}$

Mozart, *The Magic Flute*, Act II

Fig. 10.15. $\flat II$-$\sharp iii^{d7}$

Vivaldi, Concerto Grosso, Op. 3, No. 6

The Neapolitan sixth chord may be preceded by its secondary dominant in major, the $\flat VI$ (previously identified as a "borrowed" chord), and in minor, the diatonic VI triad. The alternate terminology is V of $\flat II_6$ or V of N_6.

Fig. 10.16.

Mozart, Quintet for Clarinet and Strings, K. 581, fourth movement

When found as a secondary dominant seventh chord, the seventh of the chord is chromatically lowered in relation to the key signature, $\flat VI^{-7}$ in major and VI^{-7} in minor (V^7 of N_6). In the example from Figure 10.17, the secondary dominant is used as an embellishing passing chord, $\flat II_6$-VI^{-7}-$\flat II$.

Fig. 10.17.   Chopin, Prelude, Op. 28, No. 16

The secondary leading tone triad or seventh chord to the Neapolitan sixth is occasionally encountered ($i°$-$\flat II_6$ or i^{d7}-$\flat II_6$). Here in Figure 10.18, $i°$ is used as a passing chord between $\flat II$ and $\flat II_6$. Note also the Vof$\flat II$ (VI) preceding the progression.

Fig. 10.18.   Chopin, Prelude, Op. 28, No. 12

Examples of the Neapolitan chord with root in bass, but not embellished as in the previous two examples, are occasionally seen in the early part of the historical period under study, but become fairly frequent in the middle and late nineteenth century.

Fig. 10.19.

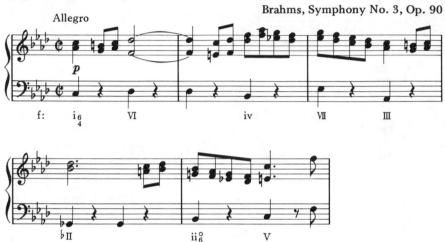

Brahms, Symphony No. 3, Op. 90

Allegro
p
f: i 6 4
VI
iv
VII
III
♭II
ii°6
V

Less Common Altered Chords

Except for chords containing thirds other than major and minor thirds, we have completed presentation of those altered chords most commonly used in the seventeenth through nineteenth centuries. But, as stated in Chapter 6, any chord can, in theory, be found with any variety of alteration, and in examining music, occasional examples of such chords will be encountered. These may occur as isolated examples as in Figures 10.20 and 10.21. In the latter figure, observe that the VI^{-7} (a dominant seventh chord above the sixth scale degree in minor) does not function here as a secondary dominant, as it did in Figure 10.17, since the root movement to the diatonic $ii^{\circ 7}$ is that of a diminished fifth.

Fig. 10.20. ♭VII, major key

Haydn, *The Creation*

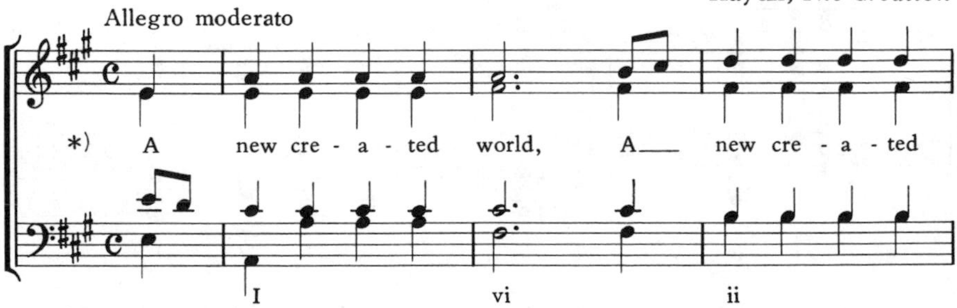

Allegro moderato
*) A new cre - a - ted world, A___ new cre - a - ted
I
vi
ii

***) Choral parts only**

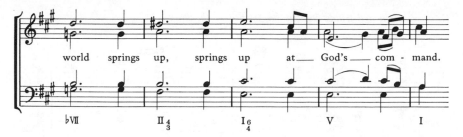

world springs up, springs up at____ God's ____ com - mand.

$\flat$VII   II$\frac{4}{3}$ I$\frac{6}{4}$ V   I

Fig. 10.21. VI^{-7}, minor key

Chopin, Mazurka No. 17, Op. 24, No. 4

Moderato

i   ii$^{\circ 7}$ $\sharp$iv^{d7} II

VI^{-7} ii$^{\circ 7}$ i

The less common altered chords appear freely over a chromatic bass line. Throughout this text we have observed the freedom of chord succession above a chromatic bass line. These have been shown in examples of short duration. Longer chromatic bass lines provide even greater opportunity for non-functional successions of chords. A chord-by-chord analysis of these sonorities often reveals a strange succession of chord numbers. In this situation, these numbers are really meaningless; the progression of sonorities is under the control of the chromatic bass line rather than by a system of root movements. In Figure 10.22, the progression is basically I-IV-iii-IV-V-I; the IV-iii-IV is in itself less common, and each of these is treated in two or three different chromatic alterations.

Fig. 10.22.

Mozart, Symphony No. 40 in G Minor, K. 550

Andante

V^7 I   iv^{-7} $\sharp$iv^{d7} $\flat$III$_6$ iii$^{d7}_{\frac{6}{5}}$

iv₆   ♯iv°₆   (♯iv^{d7})   I⁶₄   V⁷   I

One of the best known examples of the descending chromatic bass line, this one of ten measures' duration, is Chopin's Prelude in E Minor, the first part of which is shown as Figure 10.23. It should first be recognized that the right-hand "melody" is probably a pedal point on B, with an upper neighbor, in measures 1–4, and on A until measure 8. The beginning harmony and that of the cadences is clear:

$$\text{e:}\quad \text{i}\text{———}\text{I}^7\text{———}\text{iv—V iv V iv V—i}$$
$$\text{measures:}\quad 1\qquad\quad 4\qquad\qquad 9\quad 10\quad 11\quad 12\ 13$$

Between these points, the harmonic succession is controlled by the chromatic bass line, and where this is static, as in measures 4–5, by the chromatically descending inner voice. No chord-by-chord analysis can be meaningful in progressions such as these.

Fig. 10.23.

Chopin, Prelude in E Minor, Op. 28, No. 4

Assignment 10.5. Harmonic analysis.   Copy out excerpts below as assigned. Write harmonic analysis below staff.

Bach: *371 Chorales*

> No. 216, eighth phrase (chromatic bass)
> No. 310, last phrase (chromatic bass)

Beethoven: Sonatas for Piano

> No. 5 (Op. 10, No. 1), second movement, measures 31–36 (augmented triad)
> No. 14 (Op. 27, No. 2), first movement, measures 19–23 (♭II)
> No. 16 (Op. 31, No. 1), second movement, measures 27–34 (augmented triad); measures 36–41 (♭II)
> No. 17 (Op. 31, No. 2), first movement, measures 54–62 (♭II); third movement, measures 8–15 (♭II)

Chopin: Mazurkas

> No. 6 (Op. 7, No. 2), measures 9–16 (♭II)
> No. 8 (Op. 7, No. 4), measures 9–14 (♭II)
> No. 35, (Op. 56, No. 3), measures 5–9 (♭II)

Mendelssohn: *Songs Without Words*

> No. 13 (Op. 38, No. 1), measures 26–28 (♭II)
> No. 42 (Op. 85, No. 6), measures 36-40 (♭II)
> No. 20 (Op. 53, No.2), measures 5–7 (augmented triad)

Mozart, Sonata for Piano in B♭ Major, K. 281, third movement, measures 10–14 (augmented triad)

Schumann, *Album for the Young*, Op. 68, No. 34, measures 1–3 (augmented triad)

APPLICATION

Written Materials

Augmented Triads

The augmented triad is usually found with root in bass and root doubled, or in first inversion with the third doubled.

Assignment 10.6. Part-writing. Fill in alto and tenor voices. Write in harmonic analysis below staff.

The Neapolitan Sixth Chord

In four-part writing, this triad is usually found with the third doubled. Use of the fifth as a soprano note is quite rare except in an arpeggiated soprano line or in a resolution other than to tonic six-four or to the dominant.

When the root is in the bass, the root is ordinarily doubled.

Fig. 10.24.

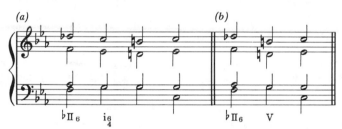

Assignment 10.7. Part-writing. Fill in alto and tenor voices. Write in harmonic analysis below staff.

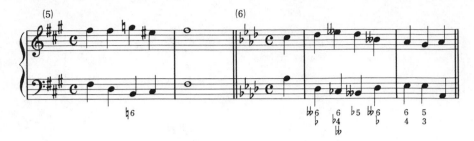

Assignment 10.8. Part-writing. These extended exercises include both augmented triads and the Neapolitan sixth chord.

Assignment 10.9. Part-writing. Write the following progressions in four parts. Choose a meter and rhythmic pattern which will insure good harmonic rhythm and correct rhythm at the cadences. Unaltered chords may be repeated if necessary.

   a) D minor i III$+_6$ VI ii$^\circ_6$ i$_6$ V i

   b) F minor i v$_6$ VI ♭II$_6$ V^7 i ii$^\circ_6$ V i

   c) E major I I$+$ ii$_6$ V^7 III$_6$ vi V V$+$ I

Assignment 10.10. Part-writing.   Write original exercises in four voices using triads and seventh chords presented in Chapters 9 and 10. Write in one of the small forms: period, phrase group, or double period.

Assignment 10.11. Realizing a chromatic bass line.   Below are given two bass lines which proceed principally by half step. Realize these lines using conventional diatonic and altered chords and any other chords built in major and minor thirds which you might devise, and as shown in Figures 10.22 and 10.23 and accompanying discussion. Choose a time signature. Each bass note may be changed to any durational value, and each may be repeated one or more times if necessary or desirable. In writing successive chromatic chords, avoid as many leaps as possible in the upper voices, especially large leaps.

PROJECT I (cont.). *Realization of figured basses.*[3]
Assignment 10.12.

Telemann, Sonata in F Minor for Flute and Figured Bass

Assignment 10.13.   This excerpt begins with the VI triad (V of ii) in G major. Measure 5 might be analyzed in several ways. In the analysis indicated, the flat above F (beat 4) may be considered an accented chromatic passing tone.

C. P. E. Bach, Sonata in G Major for Flute and Figured Bass

---

[3]Dotted bar line in score indicates an edited ending.

Assignment 10.14. From Volume 43 of the *Bach-Gesellschaft* (complete edition of Bach's works) find Sonata No. 3 for Flute and Figured Bass, third movement, "Siciliano." (Also available in Lea Pocket Scores No. 10). Realize the figured bass of this movement as in preceding assignments.

PROJECTS III–V. Continue work in these projects, making use of all altered chords studied this far. In Projects IV and V, make use of binary and ternary forms.

Ear Training

Augmented Triads

Exercise 10.1 Singing augmented triads.

a) To sing an augmented triad from its root, sing two major thirds in succession. To sing an augmented triad from its third requires that the major third be followed by the diminished fourth. This latter interval is enharmonic with a major third and can be sung as a major third.

Fig. 10.25.

M3   M3   M3   d4(M3)

b) Sing augmented triads as in *a*), but sing with letter names when the name of the root or third is given.

Exercise 10.2. Intervals in the augmented triad. Identify aurally the intervals of the augmented fifth and the diminished fourth. These two intervals are enharmonic with the minor sixth and the major third, respectively. To identify them as the augmented fifth or the diminished fourth, it is necessary that the augmented triad be heard at the same time. Follow this procedure:

a) Listen to the interval played at the piano. Sing the interval on la.

b) Listen to the chord played at the piano. The instructor will indicate whether the root or third is in the bass.

c) Sing the triad from the root, using 1, 3, 5, 3, 1.

d) Sing the interval with the correct numbers.

e) Identify the interval by name. 1 up to 5 or 5 down to 1 will be an augmented fifth. 5 up to 1 or 1 down to 5 will be a diminished fourth.

Fig. 10.26.

(1) Listen   (2)   (3) Sing   (4)

1   3   5   1   5   1

Exercise 10.3. Spelling augmented triads and intervals in the augmented triad from dictation. Follow procedure for Exercise 10.2.

a) The letter name of the bass tone will be given; whether the bass is root or third will also be given. Spell the triad, then spell the interval.

b) The letter name of one note of the interval will be given; whether the bass is the root or third will also be given. Spell the triad and the interval. An example, in which F is the first note of the interval and the bass note is the third of the triad, follows.

Fig. 10.27.

Listen

Sing

3 1 3 5   1 5   F A C♯   F C♯

Exercise 10.4.   Singing the I+, IV+, V+, and III+ triads.

a) The tonic tone will be given, together with its letter name. Sing the tonic triad with letter names, followed by the I+ triad with letter names. Repeat this procedure with the IV+ and V+ triads.

b) Follow directions in *a)* above; after the minor tonic triad sing the III+ triad.

Fig. 10.28.

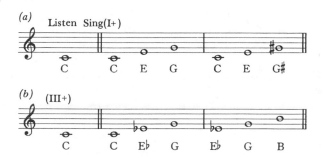

(a)   Listen Sing(I+)

C   C E G   C E G♯

(b)   (III+)

C   C E♭ G   E♭ G B

Exercise 10.5.   Singing the augmented triad in a harmonic progression. Sing the following progressions, using letter names, in keys as indicated by instructor.

I I+ IV V I
I V V+ I
I IV IV+ ii V I
i III+ VI iv V i

Exercise 10.6.   Harmonic dictation.   These exercises will now include examples of augmented triads. The root of the augmented triad can be identified positively only in the context of the surrounding harmony. Once a sonority is identified as having the sound of an augmented triad, its root will be determined by its chord of resolution.

The Neapolitan Sixth Chord

Exercise 10.7.   Sing, with letter names, the Neapolitan sixth chord in any major or minor key, as directed. Listen for the tonic note of the key; sing the tonic triad followed by the Neapolitan sixth chord.

Exercise 10.8. Harmonic dictation.   Harmonic dictation exercises will now include the Neapolitan sixth chord. The lowered second scale degree readily identifies this triad.

Keyboard Harmony

Exercise 10.9. Playing the augmented triad.   *a)* The name of the root or third of the triad will be given; spell the triad, then play the triad with root in bass or in first inversion as indicated by the given note. Double the bass note in each case.

Example: F♯ is given as the third of an augmented triad, the triad therefore to be played in first inversion. Spell D F♯ A♯.

Fig. 10.29.

b) Play the I+, IV+, V+ in major keys or the III+ in minor keys, either with root in bass or in first inversion, when the name of the key is given.

Exercise 10.10.   Play at the keyboard the following progressions:

$$I \; I+ \; IV \; V \; I$$
$$I \; I+_6 \; IV \; V \; I$$
$$I \; IV \; IV+ \; ii_6 \; V \; I$$
$$I \; V \; V+ \; I$$
$$i \; III+ \; VI \; iv \; V \; i$$
$$i \; III+_6 \; VI \; ii^\circ_6 \; i^6_4 \; V \; i$$

Exercise 10.11.   Play at the keyboard the following progressions:

$$i \; \flat II_6 \; i^6_4 \; V \; i$$
$$i \; \flat II_6 \; V \; i$$
$$I \; \flat II_6 \; I_6 \; V \; I$$
$$I \; \flat II_6 \; V^7 \; I$$
$$i \; \flat II_6 \; \sharp iv^{d7} \; i^6_4 \; V \; i$$

11

Augmented Sixth Chords

THEORY AND ANALYSIS

Chords of the augmented sixth, unlike chords previously studied, contain an interval other than a major or minor third. This interval is the diminished third, a half step smaller than a minor third. It is ordinarily found in its inverted form, the augmented sixth, hence the name of the chord (Figure 11.1*a*). There are three chord structures which include this interval, each popularly known by a geographical name.[1]

The Italian sixth—a triad consisting of a diminished third and a major third. To display the interval of the augmented sixth, the triad is found in first inversion (see Figure 11.1*b*).

The German sixth—a seventh chord consisting of a triad identical to the Italian sixth, plus the interval of a minor third above the fifth of the triad. To display the interval of the augmented sixth, the chord is found in first inversion (see Figure 11.1*c*).

The French sixth—a seventh chord consisting of the intervals of a major third, a diminished third, and a major third. To display the interval of the augmented sixth, the chord is found in second inversion (see Figure 11.1*d*).

Fig. 11.1.

| diminished | augmented | Italian sixth | German sixth | French sixth |
| third (d 3) | sixth (A 6) | | | |

---

[1]The sources or meanings of these geographical designations are unknown.

207

a) Conventional augmented sixth chords, minor keys. As used most commonly, the Italian sixth and German sixth are built on the raised fourth scale step, and the French sixth on the second scale step. When inverted to display the interval of the augmented sixth, the bass note of each chord is the sixth scale step.

Fig. 11.2.

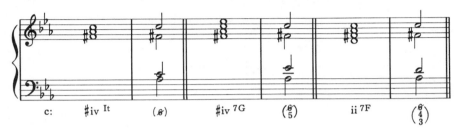

Since the triads in each of the above chords are neither major nor minor, chord symbols previously used will not suffice. In these symbols, the roman numeral will indicate the scale step upon which the chord is built; the superscript utilizes the abbreviations of the geographical name, as shown in Figure 11.2. These chords are often known by their figured bass designation—the augmented sixth chord (Italian sixth), the augmented six-five chord (German sixth), and the augmented six-four-three (French sixth). These figured bass designations are also shown in Figure 11.2.[2]

Assignment 11.1. Spell the Italian, German, and French sixth chords in each minor key. Spell each by interval, as discussed in a previous paragraph, or, first spell the diatonic chord in the key and then raise the fourth scale degree. *Examples:* (1) Spell the Italian sixth chord in D minor. The iv triad is spelled G B♭ D; raise the fourth scale step, G♯; the Italian sixth is G♯ B♭ D. (2) Spell the French sixth in G♯ minor. The ii°^{7} chord is spelled A♯ C♯ E G♯; raise the fourth scale step, C✕; the French sixth is spelled A♯ C✕ E G♯.

The interval of the augmented sixth usually resolves to an octave, the upper note of the interval progressing up a half step and the lower note down a half step. In the chords shown in Figure 11.2 this note of resolution will be the dominant note of the key. The chord at this point will usually be either V or i$_6^6$.
$_4$

---

[2] Figured bass for the French sixth chord is often given as ♭6, the ♭6 indicating an interval

$$\frac{4}{3}$$

of the augmented sixth and the ♯4 an interval of the augmented fourth. In this text, the figured bass numeral indicates the number of letter names above the bass voice, and the numeral is raised or lowered only to change an accidental in the key signature.

Fig. 11.3.

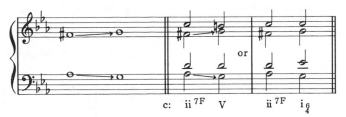

c: ii^{7F}   V   ii^{7F}   i$_4^6$

In four-voice writing, the altered tone (raised fourth scale degree) is generally approached stepwise in a non-harmonic tone figure. The sonority may be ambiguous as in Figure 11.4 where the C♯ may be analyzed as a lower neighbor in the VI⁷ chord, or the D as a suspension in the ♯iv^It.

Fig. 11.4. ♯iv^It

Bach, *Ich hab mein Sach Gott heimgestellt* (♯19)

g: ♯iv^It
       (C♯E♭G)

More definite is the four-voice following example, in which conventional resolution of the augmented sixth to both V and i₆ is shown.
                                                                    4

Fig. 11.5. ♯iv^{7G}, ♯iv^It

Lento   **Gluck, *Alceste*, Act I**

Dieux,   ren-dez nous   no-tre   roi,   no-tre   pè   -   re.

d: ♯iv^{7G}   i$_4^6$ ♯iv^It   V

Figure 11.6, written more than two hundred years later than the music of Figure 11.5, shows the same careful approach and resolution of the altered tone. This excerpt also offers examples of many altered chords studied in previous chapters: a secondary dominant chord, diminished seventh chords in succession, an augmented triad, and a Neapolitan sixth chord.

Fig. 11.6. ♯iv^{7G}

Franck, Chorale No. 2 in B Minor

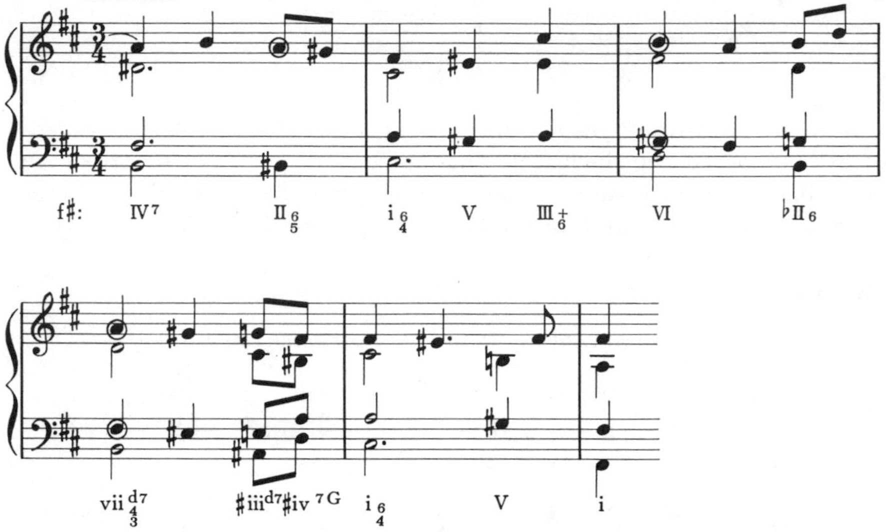

For one other example in four-voice writing, see Figure 3.4, measure 6, progression VI^7-♯iv^{It}-ii^{7F}-i_6. Two successive augmented sixth chords result from the passing tone figure F-G in the tenor voice.

These chords are used more freely in instrumental writing, two examples being shown in the following two figures. In Figure 11.7, the last thirty-second note, D, of the first measure produces a momentary Italian sixth structure.

Fig. 11.7. ♯iv^{7G}

Haydn, Symphony in G Major, "Oxford," second movement

Fig. 11.8. ii^{7F}

Verdi, *Il Trovatore*, Act II, "Stride la vampa"

b) *Conventional augmented sixth chords, major keys.* The three augmented sixth chords just presented also appear in major keys, built on the same roots and with spellings identical to those in minor keys. To achieve this identical spelling, additional tones must be altered.

Fig. 11.9.

As in minor keys, the fourth scale step is raised in each chord. In major, the sixth scale step is lowered in each chord, and, in the German sixth, the third scale step is also lowered. Resolution of the interval of the augmented sixth is identical to that found in minor keys.

Assignment 11.2.   Spell the Italian, German, and French sixth chords in each major key. An augmented sixth chord in a major key is spelled the same as in the parallel minor key. *Example:* ii⁷ᶠ in B major is identical to ii⁷ᶠ in B minor, C♯ E♯ G B. When there is no parallel minor (D♭, G♭ and C♭ major), chords must be spelled by interval.

Fig. 11.10. ♯iv^It   **Beethoven, Sonata in A Major for Piano, Op. 101,**
first movement

Fig. 11.11. ♯iv⁷ᴳ   **Mozart, Symphony in D Major,** *Prague,* **K. 504,**
second movement

Fig. 11.12. ii⁷ᶠ   **Beethoven, Sonata in A Major for Violin and Piano**
Op. 47, "Kreutzer," first movement

c) Alternate spellings of the German sixth chord in a major key. In a major key, the seventh of the ♯iv⁷ᴳ is a lowered third scale step. In resolving to I₆⁴, this note progresses upwards (Figure 11.13*a*). The chord is sometimes found with its root as the raised second scale degree, its third as a raised fourth scale degree, its fifth as a lowered sixth scale degree, and the seventh the unaltered tonic tone. With this spelling, the raised notes resolve upwards and the lowered note resolves downwards. The resulting chord is the ♯ii^{7G}. Spelled on ♯ii, the chord is usually found in second inversion so that the interval of the augmented sixth will be present. In Figure 11.13*b*) the D♯ resolves upwards to E. This chord is sometimes known as a doubly augmented six-four-three. In Figure 11.13*b*), the interval A♭-D♯ is a doubly augmented fourth.

Fig. 11.13.

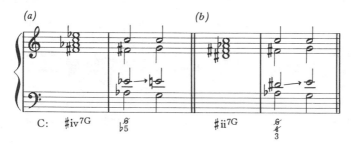

Assignment 11.3.   Spell the ♯ii^{7G} in each major key.

Fig. 11.14. ♯ii^{7G} Schumann, *Dichterliebe*, "Am leuchtenden
                                             Sommermorgen," Op. 48, No. 12

A more unusual spelling is that shown in Figure 11.15, where the German sixth chord A♯ C E G is spelled C E G B♭ in conformity with its major-minor seventh chord sound.

Fig. 11.15.   Brahms, Sonata in E Minor for Violoncello and
                                Piano, Op. 38, first movement

d) Augmented sixth chords with bass notes other than the sixth scale step. These chords are occasionally found with the root in the bass, or in some inversion other than previously described. In such cases, the interval of the diminished third often appears in the chord. This interval resolves to a unison.

Fig. 11.16. ii^{7F}, third in bass

Wagner, *Die Walküre*, Act I

Figure 11.17 includes a number of augmented sixth sonorities: (1) a "normal" German sixth chord; (2) the German sixth with root in bass; (3) a descending melodic line which creates a series of differing augmented sixth sonorities, German, French, and Italian in order, all with the raised fourth scale step in the bass, finally ending with an interval of a diminished third resolving to a unison; and (4) two additional augmented sixth chords which will be discussed under *e* below.

Fig. 11.17. ♯iv^{7G}, Root in bass

Tschaikowski, *Eugene Onegin*, Act I

The German sixth chord at the * in Figure 11.18 is not only in second inversion, but is spelled both as a $\sharp iv^{7G}$, D F♭ A♭ C♭, and as a $\sharp ii^{7G}$, B D F♭ A♭. The enharmonic pitches B and C♭ are both used as part of the chord spelling. The $V+^9$ will be discussed in Chapter 12.

Fig. 11.18. $\sharp iv^{7G}$ ($\sharp ii^{7G}$), second inversion

Wolf, *Zur Ruh, zur Ruh!*

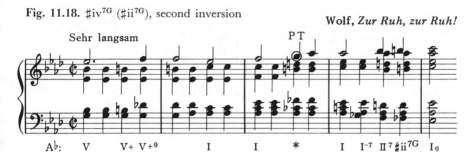

A♭:   V   V+ V+⁹   I   I   *   I   I⁻⁷ II⁷$\sharp ii^{7G}$ I$_4^6$

In Figure 11.19, the pedal point gives the aural effect of the German sixth in third inversion. The interval of the augmented sixth, B♭♭-G, resolves normally to the octave A♭.

Fig. 11.19. $\sharp ii^{7G}$ **Dvořák, Symphony No. 9 in E Minor, Op. 95,**   **"New World," second movement**

D♭:   vi   iv$_4^6$ $\sharp ii^{7G}$ I

e) Augmented sixth chords built on scale steps other than ii, $\sharp ii$, or $\sharp iv$, with normal resolution of the interval of the augmented sixth. In this category, augmented sixth chords built on the dominant and leading tone are most common.

Fig. 11.20. v^{7F} in F major = C E G♭ B♭
A6 interval G♭-E resolves to octave F

Gounod, *Faust*, Act II

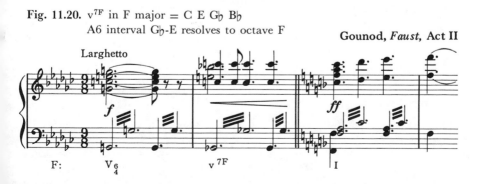

F: V$_4^6$ v ^{7F} I

Fig. 11.21. vii^{It} in C minor = B D♭ F
   A6 interval D♭-B resolves to octave C

Fauré, *Au bord de l'Eau*, Op. 8, No. 1

Fig. 11.22. vii^{7G} in E minor = D♯ F A C
   A6 interval F-D♯ resolves to octave E

W. F. Bach (1710–1784), Sonata in G Major for Piano

Fig. 11.23. iii^{7F} in F major = A C♯ E♭ G
        A6 interval E♭-C♯ resolves to octave D

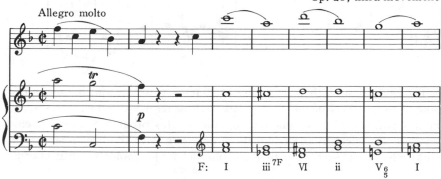

Beethoven, Sonata in A Minor for Violin and Piano,
Op. 23, third movement

In this example, the iii^{7F} precedes a secondary dominant which in turn proceeds to its temporary tonic (VI-ii or V of ii-ii). Considering the ii triad as the temporary goal of the harmonic progression, the iii^{7F} becomes a conventional ii^{7F} progressing to V and i in G minor. Compare this procedure with the principle of the extension of the secondary dominant as found in Figure 8.12 and accompanying discussion.

Two other chords are shown in an earlier illustration, Figure 11.17. Located in measure 5, they are:

♯i^{It} in C major = C♯ E♭ G, A6 interval E♭-C♯ resolves to octave D
v^{7F} in C major = G B D♭ F, A6 interval D♭-B resolves to octave C.

f) *Augmented sixth chords in which the interval of the augmented sixth does not resolve to the octave.* This group consists of augmented sixth chords spelled conventionally or unconventionally, with the additional characteristic of an irregular resolution of the interval of the augmented sixth. Such irregular resolutions are characteristic of late nineteenth-century composers.

Although the augmented sixth chord of Figure 11.24 is conventional in construction and approach, the bass note, the lower note of the interval of the augmented sixth, does not resolve down by step, but rather, leaps up a major third to the tonic of the key.

Fig. 11.24. ♯iv^{7G}

The German sixth chord of Figure 11.25 resolves to V^7 requiring the upper note of the interval of the augmented sixth to resolve downwards (A♯-A♮). Perfect parallel fifths become unavoidable in this progression; Franck emphasizes this effect by preceding the progression with the VI^7, creating the aural effect of a succession of three parallel major-minor seventh chords.

Fig. 11.25. ♯iv^{7G}-V^7

In Figure 11.26, the arpeggiated F♭ A♭ C♭ chord in the accompaniment looks like a ♭VI triad in A♭ major; the augmented sixth chord is created by the addition of D in the voice part. Resolution of the chord is interrupted by the secondary dominant II^7 (V^{7}of V).

Fig. 11.26. ♯iv^{7G}

schön sind die Haa - re, schön ist, die sie strählt!

II$_3^4$ I$_4^6$

Two unconventional chords are included in the next figure. At *a*), the chord spelling F♯ A♭ C♭ E♭ conforms to no previous spelling, though the F♯ might be considered a passing tone. At *b*), the spelling F♯ A♭ C E♭ would be a ♯ii^{7G}, this chord in first inversion to produce the interval of the augmented sixth, and not to be confused with the previously described ♯ii^{7G} (see page 212). The lower note of the interval of the augmented sixth drops a perfect fourth in its resolution.

Fig. 11.27. unconventional spelling   Gounod, *Faust,* "Introduction"

Adagio molto   (a)   (b)

E♭:   IV   I

g) Augmented seventh chords containing the interval of the augmented sixth. These chords are augmented triads with the interval of a seventh added above the root of the triad.

Fig. 11.28.

C: I+$^{-7}$ V+^{7} c: VI+$^{-7}$

These chords are infrequently used in music. Of the three, the first two are by far the more common; the VI+$^{-7}$ is shown here to illustrate a use of an augmented seventh chord which might occasionally be encountered.

Assignment 11.4. Spell the I+$^{-7}$ and the V+^{7} in each major key.

In each of these chords, the voices are usually arranged to show the interval of the augmented sixth rather than the diminished third. They differ from the augmented sixth chords in that the lower note of the interval of the augmented sixth is usually in an inner voice, as will be observed in the following illustrations.

Fig. 11.29.

Mendelssohn, *Songs Without Words*, Op. 38, No. 1

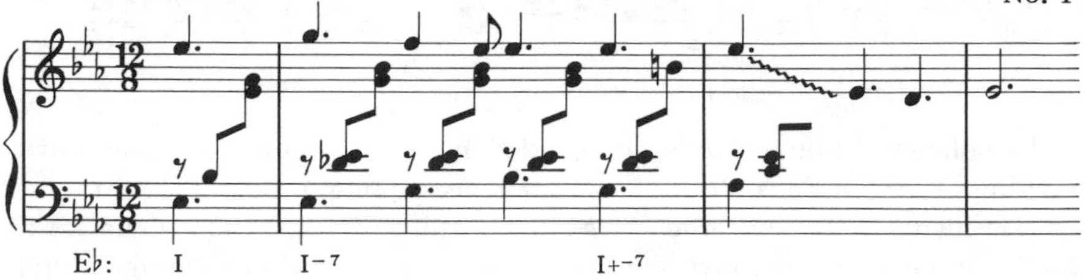

Fig. 11.30. V+⁷

d'Indy, *La Rêve de Cinyras,* Act II

Fig. 11.31. VI+⁻⁷

Franck, Chorale No. 2 in B Minor

This excerpt also shows an example of the ♯iv⁷ᴳ in third inversion. At the point of resolution, the fifth of the tonic six-four is added as a new voice, creating the aural effect of a normal resolution.

Assignment 11.5. Harmonic analysis. Copy out excerpts below as assigned. Write in chord numbers below the staff and identify non-harmonic tones. Certain excerpts list the augmented sixth chord contained therein; no identification is given in the others.

Beethoven: Sonatas for Piano

No. 4 (Op. 7), second movement, measures 72–78 (French sixth)
No. 5 (Op.10, No. 1), second movement, measures 36–42; third movement, measures 1–5
No. 6 (Op. 10, No. 2), second movement, measures 9–16
No. 8 (Op. 13), third movement, measures 44–47, 64–69

Chopin: Mazurkas

No. 2 (Op. 6, No. 2), measures 17–20
No. 35 (Op. 56, No. 3), measures 79–81 (augmented seventh)
No. 36 (Op. 59, No. 1), measures 79–82

Mendelssohn, *Songs Without Words*

No. 6 (Op. 19, No. 6), measures 22–25 (German sixth)
No. 8 (Op. 30, No. 2), measures 22–16 from end
No. 21 (Op. 53, No. 3), measures 38–44
No. 38 (Op. 85, No. 2), measures 1–5
No. 40 (Op. 85, No. 4), measures 8–5 from end (less common use)

Mozart: Sonatas for Piano

F Major, K. 280, third movement, measures 101–106 (Italian sixth)
Fantasia and Sonata, K. 475, Fantasia, measures 1–2
C Major, K. 533, first movement, measures 85–87

APPLICATION

Written Materials

The writing of an augmented sixth chord is based upon the approach and resolution of the interval of the augmented sixth.

Approach by step. Most frequently, each note of the interval is approached by whole step, by half step, or by same note. Oblique motion and contrary motion in approaching and leaving the interval are, as might be expected, most common, while similar motion is sometimes useful.

Fig. 11.32.

Oblique   Contrary   Similar

Approach by leap. The lower note of the interval may be approached by leap from the tonic note as in Figures 11.7 and 11.8. The upper note is approached by leap occasionally as in Figure 11.11. Both voices are not approached by leap at the same time.

Resolution. The interval of the augmented sixth resolves outwards to the octave.

Exceptional practices may be summarized as follows:

a) The interval of the diminished third resolves to the unison (see Figure 11.17).

b) The progression ♯iv^{7G}-V always produces perfect parallel fifths. Earlier composers usually employed the ♯iv^{It} when progressing to V (see Figure 11.5); with the ♯iv^{7G}, some evasive device was used such as is shown in Figure 11.7, where the tone located a fifth above the bass moves quickly to a tone a third above the bass, creating an Italian sixth of very short duration. Late nineteenth-century composers allowed the parallel fifths to stand (see Figure 11.25).

c) In the progression ♯iv^{7G}-V^7, both notes of the interval of the augmented sixth resolve down by half step (review Figure 11.25).

d) Members of the augmented seventh chord are so arranged that the interval of the augmented sixth is present, and this interval resolves normally (review Figures 11.29 to 11.31). The chord of resolution will contain a doubled third.

In the four-note chords (German and French sixths) no tone is doubled or omitted. In the three-note chord (Italian sixth), the fifth of the triad is doubled, since the root and third comprise the interval of the augmented sixth.

Assignment 11.6. Part-writing augmented sixth chords. These exercises contain examples of the conventional augmented sixth chords and the German sixth with alternate spelling, as described on page 212. Fill in inner voices and make harmonic analysis below the staff.

Assignment 11.7. Part-writing augmented sixth chords.   These exercises contain examples of augmented sixth chords other than those used in Assignment 11.6, as described on pages 214–217. Fill in the inner voices and make harmonic analysis below the staff.

Assignment 11.8. Part-writing augmented sixth chords: 1–4, soprano and bass given; 5–6, bass only given. These exercises contain representative examples from all the augmented sixth chords. Complete missing voices and make harmonic analysis below the staff.

Assignment 11.9. Melody harmonization.   The following melodies are taken from songs by Franz Schubert and can be found in Volume One of the songs (C. F. Peters edition or G. Schirmer edition) as follows:

    a) *Die Winterreise,* "Rast," Op. 89, No. 10, measures 26–31.
    b) *Die Winterreise,* "Der Wegweiser," Op. 89, No. 20, last line of melody.
    c) *Ständchen,* "Horch, horch, die Lerch" ("Hark, Hark, the Lark"), measures 23–30.
    d) *Der Wanderer,* Op. 4, No. 1, last line of melody.

Harmonize each melody with piano accompaniment, using an augmented sixth chord at some point. Compare your results with Schubert's accompaniment.

(1)   **Moderato**

(2) Moderato

(3) Allegretto

(4) Sehr langsam

Assignment 11.10.   Write a short original composition in chorale style or in instrumental style, making use of augmented sixth chords as studied in this chapter.

Assignment 11.11.   Continue work in projects II-V, as assigned, now using examples from all the altered chords studied in Chapters 7 to 11.

Ear Training

The interval of the augmented sixth is enharmonic with the interval of the minor seventh (Figure 11.33*a*). In listening to chords containing the interval of the augmented sixth, confusion with chords containing the interval of the minor seventh may easily result. This is particularly true in the case of the Italian and German sixth chords, each of which has a sound enharmonic with a major-minor seventh chord (Figure 11.33*b* and *c*).

Fig. 11.33.

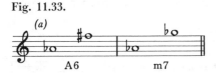

Less confusion exists with the French sixth because of the dissonant character of the sonority caused by the presence of both a major third and an augmented fourth above the bass note.

Differentiation between the augmented sixth chord sound and the major-minor seventh chord can be made by listening to the resolution of the interval in question. If the interval is an augmented sixth, the upper tone will progress *up* by half step. If the interval is a minor seventh, the upper note will progress *down* by half-step.

Exercise 11.1. Singing the interval of the augmented sixth.

a) Sing, using letter names, the interval of a minor seventh; then sing the same interval with the spelling of an augmented sixth.

Fig. 11.34.

b) Sing intervals as in *a*) above, and add the resolution of each interval.

Fig. 11.35.

Exercise 11.2. Singing augmented sixth chords.   *a*) Sing, using letter names, each of the three augmented sixth chords. Instead of singing from the root, as has been done previously, sing these chords from the bass tone usually found in an augmented sixth chord—sixth scale step in minor and lowered sixth scale step in major.

Fig. 11.36.

b) Sing augmented sixth chords as in *a*) above, but follow each chord with the dominant chord or tonic six-four, as directed, for example:

Fig. 11.37.

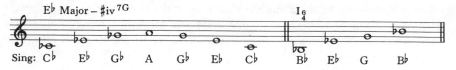

Sing: C♭   E♭   G♭   A   G♭   E♭   C♭   B♭   E♭   G   B♭

Exercise 11.3. Harmonic dictation.   Exercises in harmonic dictation will now include examples of augmented sixth chords. The following points will be helpful in identifying augmented sixth chords.

a) The German sixth sound is enharmonic with that of a complete major-minor seventh chord. Listen for the resolution of the interval of the augmented sixth. When this interval resolves out to the octave on the dominant, the chord is the ♯iv⁷ᴳ or, in a major key, may be a ♯ii⁷ᴳ. Aural discrimination between the ♯iv⁷ᴳ and ♯ii⁷ᴳ is impossible. When the interval of the augmented sixth resolves out to the tonic note of the key, the chord is vii⁷ᴳ.

b) The Italian sixth sound is enharmonic with that of an incomplete major-minor seventh chord, with the fifth of the major-minor seventh chord sound missing. When the interval of the augmented sixth resolves out to the octave of the dominant, the chord is ♯iv^It; when the interval resolves out to the tonic note, the chord is vii^It.

c) The French sixth has a dissonant sound comparable to no other chord. A chord containing the interval of the augmented sixth and which does *not* sound enharmonic with a major-minor seventh chord is a French sixth. When the interval of the augmented sixth resolves out to the dominant tone, the chord is ii⁷ᶠ; when the interval resolves out to the tonic note, the chord is V⁷ᶠ.

d) Augmented sixth chords resolving to the dominant note are the most common. Augmented sixth chords resolving to tones other than the tonic or dominant, or in a position so that the interval of the diminished third is present, are comparatively rare. Identification by ear must depend upon the special circumstances in each case.

e) After listening to the harmonic dictation exercise, sing the chords from their roots as usual, except that the augmented sixth chords should be sung as in Figure 11.36.

Keyboard Harmony

Exercise 11.4. Playing augmented sixth chords at the keyboard.   Follow this procedure.

a) Choose a key and a particular augmented sixth chord.

b) Spell the augmented sixth chord in the chosen key.

c) With the left hand, play the sixth scale degree (minor key) or lowered sixth scale degree (major key).

d) Play the remaining members of the chord with the right hand in any soprano position. Follow doubling rules stated on page 222.

Fig. 11.38.

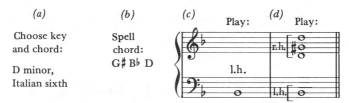

Exercise 11.5. Play an augmented sixth chord and resolve it to V or tonic six-four. Follow procedure in Exercise 11.4. Be sure the interval of the augmented sixth resolves out to the octave.

Fig. 11.39.

Exercise 11.6. Play the following progressions in keys as assigned. Each exercise contains a German sixth chord. Replay each exercise twice, substituting an Italian sixth and a French sixth in successive playings.

Minor keys

$i \; \sharp iv^{7G} \; i_6^4 \; V \; i$

$i \; VI \; \sharp iv^{7G} \; i_6^4 \; V \; i$

$i \; VI^7 \; \sharp iv^{7G} \; i_6^4 \; V \; i$

$i \; iv_6 \; \sharp iv^{7G} \; i_6^4 \; V \; i$

$i \; \sharp iv_6^{\circ} \; \sharp iv^{7G} \; i_6^4 \; V \; i$

$i \; ii_4^{\circ} {}_3 \; \sharp iv^{7G} \; i_6^4 \; V \; i$

Major keys

$I \; \sharp iv^{7G} \; I_6^4 \; V \; I$

$I \; \flat VI \; \sharp iv^{7G} \; I_6^4 \; V \; I$

$I \; IV_6 \; \sharp iv^{7G} \; I_6^4 \; V \; I$

$I \; iv_6 \; \sharp iv^{7G} \; I_6^4 \; V \; I$

$I \; \sharp iv_6^{\circ} \; \sharp iv^{7G} \; I_6^4 \; V \; I$

$I \; ii_4 {}_3 \; \sharp iv^{7G} \; I_6^4 \; V \; I$

Exercise 11.7. Play at the keyboard examples from Assignments 11.6 and 11.7.

Exercise 11.8 Harmonize the following melodic excerpts at the keyboard.

12

Chords of the Ninth, Eleventh, and Thirteenth

THEORY AND ANALYSIS

The principle of chord construction by the addition of thirds can be continued past the triad and the seventh chord to include the ninth chord, the eleventh chord, and the thirteenth chord. Chords of greater complexity are not possible, since the fifteenth above a given note is simply a repetition of the given root two octaves higher.

Fig. 12.1.

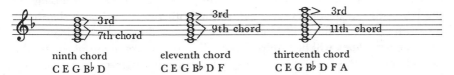

ninth chord	eleventh chord	thirteenth chord
C E G B♭ D	C E G B♭ D F	C E G B♭ D F A

Chords of the Ninth

Figure 12.2 illustrates those ninth chords which are used with some degree of regularity, the V^9 and the V^{-9} being the most common. In the construction of these chords, the root, third, and fifth forms either a major or minor triad, while the seventh is a minor seventh above the root. The roman numeral analysis number will indicate the quality of the triad and will imply a minor seventh above the root. The superscript ^{9} will indicate that the note a ninth above root will be diatonic in the key, and the superscript $^{-9}$ will indicate a ninth above the root chromatically lowered one half step.

233

Fig. 12.2.

$$F: \quad V^9 \qquad V^{-9} \qquad ii^9 \qquad \underset{V^9 \text{of } V}{II^9} \qquad \underset{V^9 \text{of } IV}{I^9} \qquad f: \quad V^9 \qquad iv^9 \qquad IV^9$$

Assignment 12.1.   *a*) Spell the V^9, V^{-9}, ii^9, II^9, and I^9 in each major key.
    b) Spell the V^9, iv^9, and IV^9 in each minor key.

It is often difficult to ascertain whether a sonority containing a ninth above the root is a ninth chord or merely a simpler chord with a non-harmonic tone. For purposes of definition, a sonority consisting only of a triad and a ninth will *not* be considered a ninth chord. The dissonances in these examples are best analyzed as simple non-harmonic tones.

Fig. 12.3.

A sonority can be considered a ninth chord with more assurance when both the ninth and the seventh are present. Since the ninth chord consists of five notes, one note is omitted in four-voice writing, usually the fifth and less often the third. In instrumental writing, the chord is often complete. In the following discussion, chords containing both the seventh and the ninth, but with either the third, fifth, or both missing, will be considered complete ninth chords. They will be grouped according to the treatment of the resolution of the ninth of the chord. Illustrations of particular ninth chords will be found as follows:

Major keys

V^9, Figures 12.13, 12.14, 12.17
V^{-9}, Figure 12.11
ii^9, Figures 12.8, 12.16

II^9, Figures 12.9, 12.15
I^9, Figures 12.10, 12.18

Minor keys

V^9, Figure 12.5
iv^9, Figure 12.6
IV^9, Figure 12.7

Less Common Ninth Chords

    VI^9, Figure 12.24
    VI^{-9}, Figure 12.19
    VII^9, Figure 12.19

The ninth chord contains two dissonances, a ninth and a seventh above the root of the chord. These are treated in the same manner as already described for the seventh of a seventh chord, that is, each of these tones is introduced as a non-harmonic tone figure (passing tone, upper neighbor, suspension or appoggiatura from below) and then resolves downwards.

Fig. 12.4.

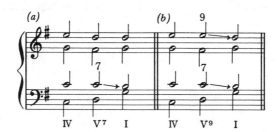

a) *Complete ninth chords in which the ninth resolves simultaneously with the chord change.* This variety of the ninth chord, though not the most frequent, can be specifically analyzed as a true harmonic sonority (as opposed to chord plus non-harmonic tone) more easily than those which follow. The ninths in the illustrations of this group show a variety of approaches: upper neighbor (Figures 12.6 and 12.8), suspension (Figure 12.7), appoggiatura (Figure 12.9), and passing tone (Figure 12.10). The first example, Figure 12.5, shows no specific note of approach since the ninth chord is the first chord of the phrase.

Fig. 12.5. V^9

Beethoven, Sonata for Violoncello and Piano, Op. 5, No. 2

The following two figures demonstrate the iv^9 and IV^9 in minor keys, the difference in the triad determined by the direction of the sixth scale step. Note also the double suspension to introduce the ninth and seventh of the IV^9.

Fig. 12.6. iv⁹

Domenico Scarlatti, Suite LXXIV (Longo 366)

Fig. 12.7. IV⁹, minor key

Clerambault(1676—1749) Suite du Premier ton
(for organ)

The ii⁹ of Figure 12.8, though non-dominant, acts as a kind of embellishing chord to the dominant triad.

Fig. 12.8. ii⁹

Grieg, *In der Heimat*

The ninth chords in each of the next two figures are examples this sonority used as a secondary dominant function, II⁹ (V⁹of V) and I⁹ (V⁹of IV).

Fig. 12.9. II⁹

Tschaikowski, *The Nutcracker,* "Overture"

Fig. 12.10. I^9

Chopin, Nocturne, Op. 72, No. 1

b) Complete ninth chords in which the ninth resolves before a change of chord. It is in this form that the complete ninth chord is most frequently found. When the ninth resolves to the octave, a seventh chord remains. This "premature" resolution is identical to that described in the discussion of the diminished seventh chord (review page 170). Analysis of this sonority as a seventh chord above which is located a non-harmonic tone is perfectly justifiable in lieu of analysis as a ninth chord.

Although only the V^{-9} is illustrated, this resolution of the ninth is very common in all ninth chords.

Fig. 12.11. V^{-9}

Schumann, *Dichterliebe*, "Ich grolle nicht," Op. 48, No. 7

c) *Complete ninth chords in which the seventh and ninth are arpeggiated.* The ninth may be resolved by leap to the seventh, 9–7 (Figure 12.12*a*), or via a passing tone to the seventh, 9–8–7 (Figure 12.12*b*). The passing tone passage is often preceded by a leap from seventh to ninth, 7–9–8–7 (Figure 12.12*c*).

Fig. 12.12.

Figures 12.13 and 12.14 illustrate the leap 9–7. The ninth chord of the latter figure is shown in first inversion, a comparatively rare occurrence.

Fig. 12.13. V⁹, leap 9–7   **Wagner,** *Goetterdaemerung,* **Act III**

Fig. 12.14. V⁹, first inversion, leap 9–7

Dvořák, Quartet, Op. 105, third movement

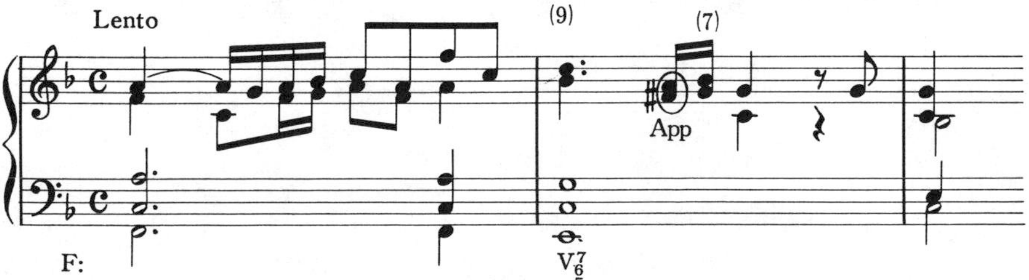

The pattern 9–8–7, accompanied by another voice a third lower, 7–6–5, is shown in Figure 12.15, and the pattern 7–9–8–7 in Figure 12.16.

Fig. 12.15. II⁹, 9–8–7

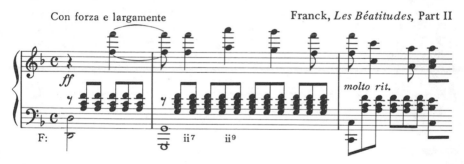

Fig. 12.16. ii⁹, 7–9–8–7

d) Complete ninth chords with irregular resolution of the ninth. Assuming the normal resolution of the ninth to be down by step, resolutions are occasionally found in which the ninth proceeds in some other way. In Figure 12.17, the ninth, D, resolves up by step. The use of this chord in third inversion is quite rare.

Fig. 12.17. V⁹

The effect of a ninth chord sonority is created by the use of an ascending accented passing tone, G, in the following example.

Fig. 12.18. I⁹   Brahms, Romance, Op. 118, No. 5

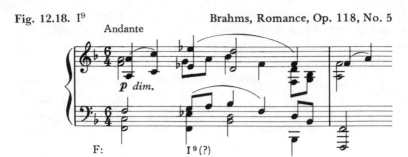

e) Ninth chords in sequence. When found in sequence, ninth chords and seventh chords are usually found alternately. Use of sequence allows the presence of ninth chords not ordinarily encountered, such as the VI⁻⁹ (V⁹of ii) and the VII⁹ (V⁹of iii) seen in Figure 12.19.

Fig. 12.19.

Tschaikowski, *Romeo and Juliet*

The aural impression of a sequence of alternating seventh and ninth chords is produced in Figure 12.20, though no complete ninth chord is present.

Fig. 12.20.   Mozart, Sonata in E♭ Major for Violin and Piano,
                                         K. 380, second movement

V^7 $i^{(9)}$ ──── $\sharp iv^{d7}=$ ──── i^6 $\sharp iv^{7}G$ V
g: vii^{d7}

Eleventh and Thirteenth Chords

Chords of the eleventh containing a ninth, and chords of the thirteenth containing an additional ninth or eleventh, are comparatively rare. Most vertical sonorities containing an eleventh or thirteenth above the bass will prove to be simply a triad or seventh chord above which is a non-harmonic tone. In Figure 12.21, the sonority could be construed to be the chord Bb (D) F Ab (C) Eb, an eleventh chord built on Bb. It is more likely that the Eb is a suspension in the Bb D F Ab chord.

Fig. 12.21.

Mendelssohn, *Songs without Words,*
Op. 53, No. 2

Allegro non troppo

eb: V^7 i

A sonority can more accurately be called an eleventh chord when the ninth is also present. Similarly, the thirteenth chord should also display either the ninth or eleventh. But even when a sonority is more positively identifiable as an eleventh or thirteenth chord, the dissonances in each almost invariably resolve while the root of the chord is being held ("premature" resolution), so that at the time of a change of root, only a more simple sonority, seventh or ninth, remains. Under these circumstances, it is difficult to assume the existence of any eleventh or thirteenth chord, when the simpler analysis of seventh or ninth chord plus dissonance is available.

Fig. 12.22.

Assuming, however, the existence of these chords, their properties can be examined. In the eleventh chord, the third is omitted since this note is the eleventh's note of resolution (Part-writing Rule 8), as in Figures 12.22*a, b,* in Figure 12.23, and in measure 8 of Figure 12.24.

Fig. 12.23. V^{11}

Mendelssohn, *Songs Without Words,*
Op. 53, No. 2

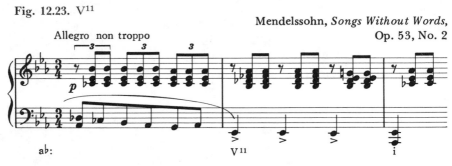

Fig. 12.24. II^{11}

Wagner, *Goetterdaemerung,* Act I

In the eleventh chord, the interval between the ninth and the eleventh may be either a third or a tenth. When the interval is a third, both the eleventh and ninth resolve down by step to a seventh chord, as in Figure 12.22*a* and Figure 12.23. When the interval is a tenth, the eleventh may resolve down by step, leaving a ninth chord, as in Figure 12.22*b* and Figure 12.25.

Fig. 12.25. V^{11}, V^{13} Duparc, *Soupir*

In the thirteenth chord, either the ninth or the seventh and the ninth together are usually present. In Figure 12.22*c*, the simultaneous resolution of the thirteenth and the eleventh produces a simple V^7 chord. The resolution of the thirteenth in Figure 12.25 leaves a V^9 sonority. In Figure 12.26, where the seventh, ninth, eleventh, and thirteenth sound simultaneously, the eleventh and thirteenth resolve in succession, leaving again a V^9 chord.

Fig. 12.26. V^{13}

Chopin, Nocturne, Op. 62, No. 1

A unique example is shown in Figure 12.27 where four chords larger than a seventh occur within the duration of three measures.

Fig. 12.27. I^{11}, ii^{11}, V^{13}

Grieg, *Spielmannslied*

Assignment 12.2. Harmonic analysis.   Copy out excerpts below, as assigned. Write in chord numbers below staff and identify non-harmonic tones.

Beethoven: Sonatas for Piano

    No. 1 (Op. 2, No. 1), first movement, measures 55–61, 89–93
    No. 14 (Op. 27, No. 2), second movement, measures 49–53

Chopin: Mazurka No. 35 (Op. 56, No. 3), measures 24–20 from end (F minor)

Mendelssohn: *Songs Without Words*

    No. 8 (Op. 30, No. 2), measures 13–18
    No. 19 (Op. 53, No. 1), measures 8–4 from end
    No. 22 (Op. 53, No. 4), measures 9–13

Mozart: Sonata for Piano in F Major, K. 332, first movement, measures 94–101; second movement, measures 5–8

Schumann: *Album for the Young,* Op. 68, No. 15, last 6 measures

APPLICATION

Written Materials

The ninth of the ninth chord is usually introduced and resolved in the manner of a non-harmonic tone. It usually resolves down, either stepwise or by skip to the seventh of the chord, and is introduced in one of five ways.

a) As a passing tone figure—See Figure 12.10.

b) As a suspension—See Figures 12.7, 12.11, 12.15.

c) As a neighboring tone—See Figures 12.6, 12.8, and 12.14.

d) As an appoggiatura, with skip from below—See Figures 12.9, 12.13, and 12.16.

e) Indeterminate introduction. In Figure 12.5, the ninth is preceded by a rest, the V^9 being the first chord following a single melodic line. In Figure 12.17, the ninth chord is the first chord in a formal motive and unrelated to the final chord of the previous measure. In Figure 12.24, the chords $\sharp i^{d7}$ and VI^9 are sonorities unrelated to each other and to the music which follows in measure 7.

Some attention must be given to placement of chord members in the vertical structure.

a) The ninth of the chord is most often found in the soprano (highest) voice. This is particularly true in ninth chords other than V^9.

b) The ninth is found at the interval of at least a ninth (rather than a second) above the root of the chord.

c) When the ninth is not the highest note, the third of the chord is almost invariably lower than the ninth (see Figure 12.5).

d) Examples of the chord with a note other than the root in the bass are uncommon (see Figure 12.14, third in bass, and Figure 12.17, seventh in bass).

The ninth chord is used only infrequently in four-voice chorale style (for example, see *Auld Lang Syne,* measure 10); it is found principally in instrumental music.

Assignment 12.3. Writing ninth chords.   These may be done for practice in four-voice chorale style, as illustrated in Figure 12.28, and in keyboard style, using Figures 12.5–12.20 for examples.

Fig. 12.28.

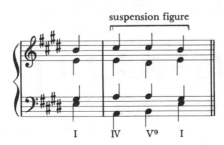

suspension figure

I   IV   V⁹   I

Write the following progressions in keys, as assigned, paying particular attention to introduction of the ninth, resolution of ninth, and placement of the third and ninth of the chord.

The ninth introduced as a suspension figure

I IV V⁹ I	i iv V⁹ i
I iv ii⁹ V⁷ I	i iv⁹ V⁷ i
I vi II⁹ V I	i IV⁹ V⁷ i
I V I II⁹ V I	
I iv V⁻⁹ I	

The ninth chord introduced as a neighboring tone

I V⁹ I	i V⁹ i
I V⁻⁹ V⁷ I	

The ninth chord introduced as an appoggiatura

I V V⁹ I	i V V⁹ i
I vi ii⁹ V I	i iv⁹ V⁷ i
I II⁹ V I	

Assignment 12.4.   Write a short original exercise in chorale or instrumental style, illustrating the use of a ninth chord.

Keyboard Harmony

Exercise 12.1.   Play at the keyboard the progressions listed in Assignment 12.3. In the ninth chords, the fifth may be omitted for ease in playing; see example in Figure 12.29. Play in all keys.

Exercise 12.2.   Play the harmonic sequence started in Figure 12.30, alternating ninth chords and seventh chords. Continue the sequence to a point where a cadence can be made on the tonic triad. Play in other major keys as directed.

Fig. 12.29.

I   IV   V⁹   I

Fig. 12.30.

I   ii⁹   V⁷   I⁹   IV⁷   vii°⁹   iii⁷   and so on

13

Advanced Modulation

THEORY AND ANALYSIS

The study of modulation more complex than that presented in Chapter 1 includes

a) modulation to closely related keys by common chord, using those seventh chords and altered chords studied in Chapters 6–11, and

b) modulation by any method to remote keys. A key in a remote relationship to a given key is one which is not closely related to the given key. The key signature of a remote key always contains at least two accidentals more or less than that of the original key.

Common Chord Modulation

a) *The diminished seventh chord as the pivot chord.* The diminished seventh chord is used extensively by all composers of the period as a pivot in modulation. Its versatility is shown by the fact that any single diminished seventh chord in a key can be used as a pivot in modulating to any other possible major or minor key. Table 13.1 demonstrates this by choosing vii^{d7} in C major. This chord, B D F A♭, and its inversions all have the same sound, so the inversions can be respelled, each with the lowest note becoming the root, and taking advantage of enharmonic spellings where available. Thus, the first inversion of B D F A♭ is D F A♭ B; by calling D the root, the chord may be spelled D F A♭ C♭, or its enharmonic equivalent C✕ E♯ G♯ B. These and the respellings of the other inversions of this chord are shown in the left hand column of Table 13.1. Since there are three different diminished seventh chord sounds in each major and minor key, each of the spellings in the left hand column may equal any one of these three different sounds, as demonstrated in the remaining columns of Table 13.1.

Any other diminished seventh chord in C major or C minor can be used to construct such a table; also, any diminished seventh chord in any other key may be used as a basis for a similar table of modulations.

TABLE 13.1.

THE DIMINISHED SEVENTH CHORD AS A PIVOT CHORD

Modulation to all major and minor keys from C
major or C minor using the vii^{d7}, B D F A♭,
as the pivot chord.

vii^{d7} in C spelled as		Major Key	Minor Key
B D F A♭	=	$\sharp iv^{d7}$ in F major	$\sharp iv^{d7}$ in F minor
	=	$\sharp i^{d7}$ in B♭ major	$\sharp iii^{d7}$ in G minor
D F A♭ C♭	=	vii^{d7} in E♭ major	vii^{d7} in E♭ minor
	=	$\sharp iv^{d7}$ in A♭ major	$\sharp iv^{d7}$ in A♭ minor
	=	$\sharp i^{d7}$ in D♭ major	$\sharp iii^{d7}$ in B♭ minor
C⁑ E♯ G♯ B	=		vii^{d7} in D♯ minor
	=		$\sharp iv^{d7}$ in G♯ minor
	=	$\sharp i^{d7}$ in C♯ major	$\sharp iii^{d7}$ in A♯ minor
F A♭ C♭ E♭♭	=	vii^{d7} in G♭ major	
	=	$\sharp iv^{d7}$ in C♭ major	
E♯ G♯ B D	=	vii^{d7} in F♯ major	vii^{d7} in F♯ minor
	=	$\sharp iv^{d7}$ in B major	$\sharp iv^{d7}$ in B minor
	=	$\sharp i^{d7}$ in E major	$\sharp iii^{d7}$ in C♯ minor
G♯ B D F	=	vii^{d7} in A major	vii^{d7} in A minor
	=	$\sharp i^{d7}$ in G major	$\sharp iii^{d7}$ in E minor
	=	$\sharp iv^{d7}$ in D major	$\sharp iv^{d7}$ in D minor

Only the three principal diminished seventh chords in each major and minor key are included in this table. Alternate functions such as $\sharp v^{d7}$ or $\sharp ii^{d7}$ are omitted here, but can be used as well in addition to those above. For example, vii^{d7} (B D F A♭) in C major = $\sharp v^{d7}$ (B D F A♭) in E♭ major.

In Figure 13.1, the second inversion of B D F A♭ (vii^{d7} in C) is respelled E♯ G♯ B D and assigned the function of $\sharp iii^{d7}$ in C♯ minor.

Fig. 13.1.

$$C: \quad I \qquad I_6 \qquad vii^{d7}_{\frac{4}{3}} =$$
$$\qquad\qquad\qquad\qquad\qquad c\sharp: \quad \sharp iii^{d7} \qquad iv \qquad V \qquad i$$

Assignment 13.1. Make a table similar to Table 13.1: *a*) in which the pivot chord is $\sharp iv^{d7}$ in C major or $\sharp iv^{d7}$ in C minor; *b*) in which $\sharp i^{d7}$ in C major is the pivot chord; *c*) in which $\sharp iii^{d7}$ in C minor is the pivot chord.

Assignment 13.2. Make tables modeled on Table 13.1 and those from Assignment 13.1 for keys other than C major or C minor, as assigned.

A modulation in which the pivot chord is spelled enharmonically is often known as an *enharmonic modulation.* The enharmonic pivot chord is usually spelled only as it functions in the new key; spelling the enharmonic pivot in both keys, as in Figures 13.1 and 13.2, is not common. When the pivot is spelled the same in both keys, as in Figure 13.3, there is no problem. The pivots of Figures 13.4–13.6 are spelled only in the new key, while Figure 13.7 shows an exceptional practice, a pivot chord whose spelling does not conform to its function in either key. Such unconventional spellings can usually be attributed to the composer's desire to simplify the spelling of the pivot.

Fig. 13.2.

Beethoven, Sonata for Piano, No. 29, Op. 106

F$\sharp$ major, viid7, E$\sharp$ G$\sharp$ B D =
E$\flat$ major, viid7, $\qquad$ D F A$\flat$ C$\flat$, both spellings shown.

$$I^6_4 \qquad\qquad\qquad vii^{d7}_2 =$$
$$\qquad\qquad\qquad\qquad E\flat: vii^{d7} \quad I$$

$$\flat VI =$$
$$F\sharp: IV \qquad V \qquad\qquad I$$

Fig. 13.3.

D major, #id7,   D# F# A C =   Haydn, Symphony in D Major *(Clock)*
A major, #ivd7, D# F# A C,   same spelling in both keys

Fig. 13.4.

C# minor, #iiid7, E# G# B D   Beethoven, *Fidelio*, Act II
C major, viid7   B D F A♭, second spelling shown

Fig. 13.5.

C♭ major, #id7   C E♭ G♭ B♭♭ =   Beethoven, Symphony No. 3 in E♭ Major, Op. 55,
E♭ minor, #ivd7, A C E♭ G♭,   second spelling shown   first movement

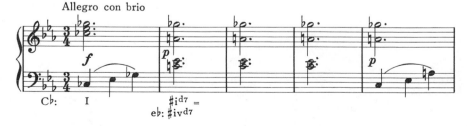

V⁷ ... i

Fig. 13.6.

C# minor, #ivd7, F✗ A# C# E =   Haydn Quartet in C Major, Op. 74, No. 1,
G major, #ivd7,   C# E G Bb, second spelling shown   second movement

c#:   i   VI   #ivd7 =   I⁶₄
               G: #ivd7

V   I

Fig. 13.7. unconventional spelling

Bb minor, viid7, A C Eb Gb =   Brahms, Trio in B Major, Op. 8,
B major, #vid7, G✗ B# D# F#,   but spelled   third movement
         D# F# A C

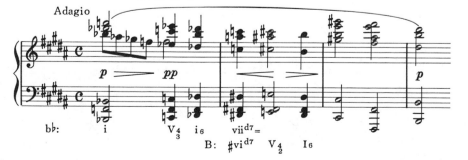

bb: i   V⁴₃   i⁶   viid7 =
                 B: #vid7   V⁴₂   I⁶

Another modulation of this type may be seen in Figure 12.20 where ♯iv^d7 of C minor = vii^d7 of G minor.

It will be recalled from Chapter 9 that the seventh of a diminished seventh chord often resolves before the resolution of the chord as a whole (premature resolution), resulting in a dominant seventh chord (e.g., B D F A♭-B D F G). This principle is sometimes extended to other members of the diminished seventh chord to produce various dominant seventh chords useful in modulatory situations. Using the same B D F A♭ chord as an example,

lowering the root B to B♭ produces	B♭ D F A♭
or	A♯ C× E♯ G♯
lowering the third D to D♭ produces	D♭ F A♭ C♭
or	C♯ E♯ G♯ B
lowering the fifth F to F♭ produces	F♭ A♭ C♭ E♭♭
or	E G♯ B D.

Each of these may be used as a dominant seventh or any secondary dominant seventh in the new key.

In Figure 13.8, the root of the vii^d7 is lowered, E♯ G♯ B D to E G♯ B D, the latter becoming the dominant seventh of the new key. This illustration shows only the harmonic skeleton of the composition. For the full pianistic figuration, and for the definite establishment of each of the two keys involved, F♯ minor and A major, refer to measures 71–109 of the sonata quoted.

Fig. 13.8.   Beethoven, Sonata No. 15 in D Major for Piano,
                                        Op. 28, first movement

In the excerpt from *Siegfried*, Figure 13.9, the composer uses this device repeatedly in short motives in close succession. The motive, first appearing in measures 1–2, begins with a half diminished seventh chord, at (1), whose seventh resolves down to create a diminished seventh chord (2), one member of which resolves down a half step to create a dominant seventh chord (3). No attempt is made to resolve the dominant seventh chord except as it progresses into another similar motive. The music of this figure continues in this manner for a total of nineteen measures.

Fig. 13.9.

Wagner, *Siegfried*, Act III

b) The German sixth chord as the pivot chord.   The sound of this chord, when found normally in first inversion, is enharmonic with that of a major-minor seventh chord. For this reason, it is a convenient chord to use as a pivot in reaching a remote key quickly. As a pivot, the German sixth chord may equal any function of a major-minor seventh chord, or, any major-minor seventh chord may equal a German sixth chord.[1] With few exceptions, however, such pivotal uses are limited to the following:

$$\sharp\text{iv}^{7\text{G}} = \text{V}^7 \qquad\qquad \text{V}^7 = \sharp\text{iv}^{7\text{G}}$$
$$\text{I}^{\ 7}\ (\text{V}^7\text{of IV}) = \sharp\text{iv}^{7\text{G}}$$

---

[1] Also, the Italian sixth may equal an incomplete major-minor seventh chord, or vice versa, but such pivots are less common.

Fig. 13.10.

(a)

(b)

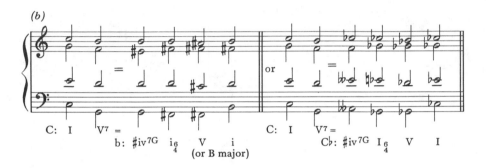

(c)

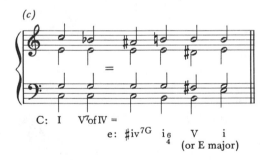

Figure 13.11 is a rare example in which both spellings of the pivot are given by the composer. Most often, as already stated, an enharmonic pivot is spelled only in the new key (Figures 13.12 and 13.13). Exceptions are shown in Figure 13.14 where the pivot is spelled in the original key, and in Figure 13.15, which uses an uncommon chord (IV^{-7} or V^7 of $\flat VII$) spelled in the original key.

Fig. 13.11.   Chopin, Mazurka, Op. 46 No. 1

B major, I⁻⁷   B D♯ F♯ A =
E♭ major, ♯iv7G, A C♭ E♭ G♭   both spellings shown

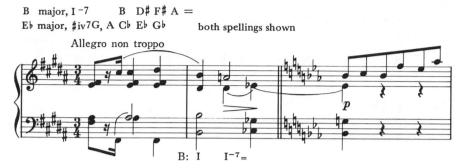

B: I   I⁻⁷=
E♭: ♯iv⁷G   I⁶₄

Fig. 13.12.

Schubert, Sonata for Piano, Op. 42,
                                              first movement

B♭ major, V7   F A C E♭ =
A minor, ♯iv7G, D♯ F A C   second spelling shown

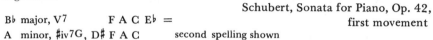

B♭:   I   V⁷=
        a: ♯iv⁷G   i   V   i

Fig. 13.13.

Beethoven, Sonata for Piano, No. 27, Op. 90,
                                              second movement

C minor, ♯iv7G, F♯ A♭ C E♭   =
C♯ minor, V7,   G♯ B♯ D♯ F♯   second spelling shown

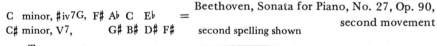

c: ii⁰₆   ♯iv d7   i ⁶₄   ♯iv ⁷G =   i
                            c♯: V⁷   3

Fig. 13.14.

Berlioz, *Les Nuits d'Été*, Op. 7, "L'Ille inconnue"

D♭ major, V7,   A♭ C E♭ G♭ =
C major, ♯iv7G, F♯ A♭ C E♭   first spelling shown

Fig. 13.15.

Mussorgsky, *Boris Gudonov*, Act III

E major, IV⁻⁷   A C♯ E G =
D♭ major, ♯iv7G, G B♭♭ D♭ F♭   first spelling shown

Assignment 13.3. Spell augmented sixth chords as enharmonic equivalents in these pivots: ♯iv⁷ᴳ = V⁷, V⁷ = ♯iv⁷ᴳ and I⁻⁷ (V⁷ofIV) = ♯iv⁷ᴳ

Examples:

    A♭ or a♭: ♯iv⁷ᴳ, D F♭ A♭ C♭ = A or a: V⁷, E G♯ B D
    B or b: V⁷, F♯ A♯ C♯ E = B♭ or b♭: ♯iv⁷ᴳ, E G♭ B♭ D♭
                  = a♯: ♯iv⁷ᴳ, D✕ F♯ A♯ C♯
    D or d: I⁻⁷ (V⁷ofIV), D F♯ A C = F♯ or f♯: ♯iv⁷ᴳ, B♯ D F♯ A
                  = G♭: C E♭♭ G♭ B♭♭

Observe that in each case the seventh of V⁷ or I⁻⁷ is the same pitch as the root of the German sixth chord.

    c) Other modulations by pivot chord. Any chord, altered or unaltered, may function as a pivot. It may be altered or diatonic in either key, or may be altered in both keys, and in addition may display enharmonic spelling. The excerpt in Figure 13.16 shows this combination: an altered chord in the original key ($\flat\text{II}_6$) which equals a diatonic chord in the new key (IV_6), with the enharmonic spelling of the new key shown. See also Figure 13.2, measure 3.

Fig. 13.16.

B♭ minor, ♭II, C♭ E♭ G♭ =

F♯ major, IV, B D♯ F♯   second spelling shown

Mozart, Symphony No. 39 in E♭ Major, K. 543, fourth movement

Modulation by Change of Mode

Since the key signature of a major key and its parallel minor differ by three accidentals, use of chords from the opposite mode will often conveniently and dramatically expedite a modulation from a major key to one of its remote keys. Most such modulations are made from a major key to a minor key, and of these, the use of a minor tonic triad in a major key is probably the single most useful vehicle for this type of modulation.

The two excerpts from Beethoven, Figures 13.17 and 13.18, demonstrate the effectiveness of this device. Changing the F major tonic triad to an F minor triad in Figure 13.17 immediately adds three flats to the original key of one flat, making entrance into the key of five flats nothing more complex than a modulation to a closely related key. The same is true of Figure 13.18, where the change from a D♭ major tonic triad (five flats) to a D♭ minor triad (eight flats) is spelled enharmonically as C♯ minor to become a vi triad in the new key.

Fig. 13.17.

F major to
D♭ major

Beethoven, Symphony No. 3, first movement

Fig. 13.18.

D♭ major, i, D♭ F♭ A♭ =
E major, vi, C♯ E G♯   second spelling shown

Beethoven, Sonata for Piano, No. 31, Op. 110,
first movement

Chords other than the tonic of the original key occasionally serve this purpose, as in Figure 13.19 where the ♭VI of B♭ major (VI of B♭ minor) becomes the tonic of G♭ major.

Fig. 13.19.

Direct Modulation

As with closely related keys, modulation to a remote key may be accomplished without benefit of a pivot (review Chapter 1), both as a new phrase, as in Figure 13.20,

Fig. 13.20.

Ab major to
F# minor   Schubert, *Moments musicals,* Op. 94, No. 2

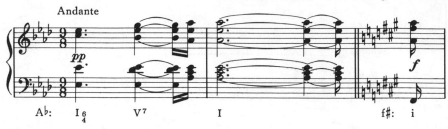

Ab: I $\frac{6}{4}$ V⁷   I   f#:   i

I⁷   iv $\frac{6}{4}$

or by chromatic half step in one of the melodic lines. In fact, many examples of modulations shown earlier in this chapter might be considered direct because of this latter feature, as in Figure 13.3, bass line D-D♯, or in Figure 13.17, inner voice A-A♮.

Very often the keys involved in a direct modulation are connected by a single pitch common to the two keys. Though this type of modulation by *pivot pitch* can be used to connect any two keys, it is used most commonly between two keys in remote relationship. The pivot pitch may be spelled the same in both keys, as in Figure 13.21, or may be spelled enharmonically, as in Figure 13.22.

Fig. 13.21.

E major to
G major   Smetana, *The Moldau*
Pivot pitch—E (root of I in E major= 5th of ii, A C E,in
                                      in G major)

E: I

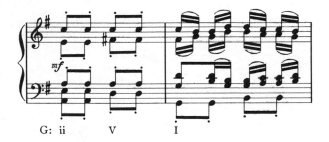

G: ii   V   I

Fig. 13.22.

B♭ minor to   Wagner, *Tristan und Isolde,* Act I
F♯ minor

Pivot pitch spelled enharmonically, D♭ - C♯ (D♭, third of tonic
triad in B♭ minor = C♯, fifth of tonic triad in F♯ minor)

Modulation by Sequence

A new key may be reached as the result of a sequence, either harmonic
or formal. Figure 13.23 shows a sequence of major-minor seventh chords
(secondary dominants); the sequence is continued until the desired key of
F major is reached. In Figure 13.24, the repetition of a two-measure phrase,
each time a major second lower, takes the music from B major to G major.

Fig. 13.23.

D minor to
F major

Mozart, Symphony No. 41 in C Major, K. 551,
second movement

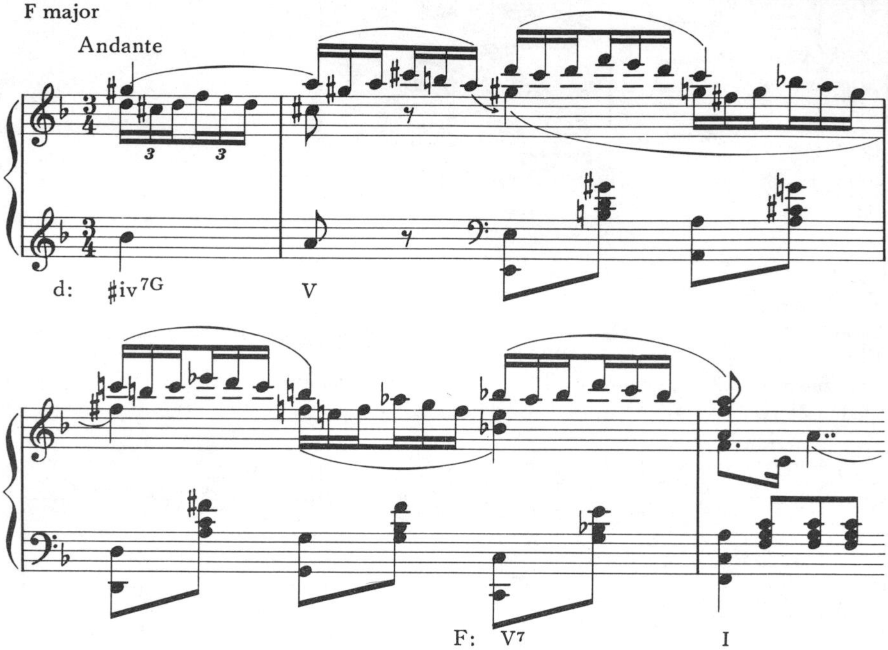

Fig. 13.24.

B major to
G major

Chopin, Mazurka, Op. 56, No. 1

A more developed use of this type of modulation is shown in Figure 13.25, which also includes modulation by pivot pitch and by change of mode.

Measure 4	pivot pitch modulation from F major to D♭ major, via the pitch F.
Measures 5–7	a three-measure motive ending on V^7 of IV (I^{-7}) (D♭ F A♭ C♭) spelled enharmonically as C♯ E♯ G♯ B, to function as V^7 in F♯ minor.
Measures 8–9	a truncated two-measure version of measures 5–7 in F♯ minor.
Measures 10–11	measures 8–9 repeated in G major.
Measure 12	the previous motive truncated to one measure and modulating to the final goal of D major.

Fig. 13.25.   Brahms, Concerto for Violin, Violoncello and
                                Orchestra, Op. 102, second movement

Passing Modulations and False Modulations

Passing modulation.   In reaching a desired key from a given key, composers often modulate to an intermediate key or keys before arriving at the cadence in the new key. These intervening modulations are known as passing modulations.

False modulation.   When a phrase begins and ends in the same key, and a modulation occurs within the phrase, the modulation is known as a false modulation.

Passing modulations and false modulations are usually very short. The aural impression of a new tonic center may vary from a tonic definitely established to one merely suggested.

Figure 13.4 shows a modulation from F minor to C major, within which is a passing modulation to C♯ minor. The passing modulation has a duration of only three chords—iii (pivot)-V-i.

Figure 13.2 shows a phrase in F♯ major, continuing a false modulation to E♭ major. Though consisting only of the progression vii^{d7}-I, the impression of E♭ is enhanced by the repetition of the E♭ triad.

Assignment 13.4. Analysis of modulations.   Locate and describe the modulation or modulations in each of the following excerpts.

Beethoven: Sonatas for Piano

   No. 5 (Op. 10, No. 1), fourth movement, measures 11–7 from end
   No. 6 (Op. 10, No. 2), first movement, measures 13–18
   No. 11 (Op. 22), second movement, measures 15–18; 31–39; 58–65; fourth movement, measures 67–72

Chopin: Mazurkas

   No. 19 (Op. 30, No. 2), measures 17–24
   No. 23 (Op. 33, No. 2), measures 45–73
   No. 25 (Op. 33, No. 4), measures 153–162
   No. 34 (Op. 56, No. 2), measures 37–44
   No. 36 (Op. 59, No. 1), measures 79–94

Mendelssohn: *Songs Without Words*

No. 2 (Op. 19, No. 2), measures 17–21
No. 10 (Op. 30, No. 4), measures 42–46
No. 19 (Op. 53, No. 1), measures 11–24

Mozart: Sonatas for Piano

B♭ Major, K. 333, third movement, measures 69–76
D Major, K. 311, third movement, measures 109–119
Fantasia and Sonata, K. 475, Fantasia, measures 23–26

Schumann: *Album for the Young,* Op. 68

No. 12, measures 25–48
No. 31, measures 1–17

APPLICATION

Written Materials

Assignment 13.5. Part-writing.   Fill in alto and tenor voices. Make harmonic analysis, including the dual function of the pivot chord in the modulation.

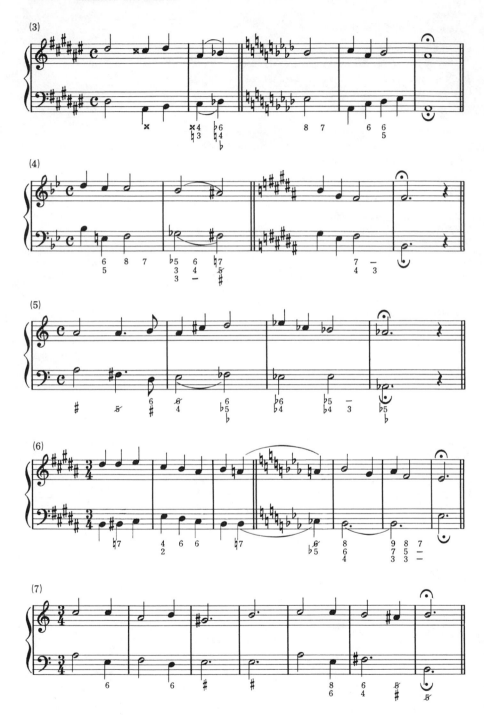

Assignment 13.6. Writing modulations between two keys with a diminished seventh chord as a pivot, and with the pivot chord given.

a) The pivot spelled in the new key and with root in bass. This is the easiest way to write a diminished seventh chord pivot. Any chord chosen as a diminished seventh in the new key can be analyzed as a usable function in the old key. In Figure 13.26, modulation from C major to B♭ minor, the ♯iii^{d7}, root in bass, functions as vii^{d7}, third in bass, in the original key.

Fig. 13.26.

C: I   vii^{d7}=
        b♭: ♯iii^{d7} iv   V   i

Any abruptness in the sound of this or any similar modulation can be softened by the use of non-harmonic tones. The music of Figure 13.27 is that of Figure 13.26, rewritten with non-harmonic tones.

Fig. 13.27.

b) The pivot in inversion in the new key. When for any reason the pivot as spelled in the new key is in inversion, each note of the diminished seventh resolves by step or remains stationary, with, of course, the root resolving up and the seventh resolving down. The harmonic progression of Figure 13.28 is the same as that of Figure 13.26. The vii^{d7} of C major is in root position, which, when respelled in B♭ minor, is found as the third inversion of the ♯iii^{d7}. It resolves to a iv$_6$, which in turn resolves as a pedal six-four to the tonic triad.

Fig. 13.28.

In writing modulations of this kind, an awkward melodic interval may appear in approaching the diminished seventh chord. Again, a judicious use of non-harmonic tones ordinarily will correct the situation.

Fig. 13.29.

dim. 3rd

In the following exercises, the chord in parentheses is the pivot chord as spelled in the *original* key. Write each exercise, as assigned, in two ways: (1) the pivot with root in bass as respelled in the new key (Figure 13.26) and (2) the pivot with root in bass as spelled in the original key, but respelled in the new key (Figure 13.28). Use non-harmonic tones where necessary or desirable.

C major (vii^{d7}) to A♭ major
C major (♯iv^{d7}) to F major
G minor (♯iii^{d7}) to F major
B minor (vii^{d7}) to d minor
A major (♯i^{d7}) to G♭ major
D♭ major (♯v^{d7}) to E♭ major
F♯ minor (vii^{d7}) to C minor
E♭ minor (♯iv^{d7}) to F minor
F♯ major (♯i^{d7}) to A major
A♭ minor (vii^{d7}) to B♭ major

Assignment 13.7. Writing modulations between two keys with a diminished seventh chord as pivot, but the pivot chord not given.

a) Write out the following modulations

C major to A♭ major
E major to B♭ major
E minor to C♯ minor
G minor to E major
F♯ major to A♭ major
D♯ minor to G major

b) Choose other pairs of keys and write out appropriate modulation.

Assignment 13.8. Writing modulations between two keys making use of the premature resolution of any tone of the diminished seventh chord. Choose a diminished seventh chord in the original key and, in separate exercises, resolve each note of the diminished seventh chord prematurely, modulating to an appropriate key. Review Figures 13.8 and 13.9, and accompanying discussion. In the Keyboard Harmony section of this chapter, consult Figure 13.30.

Assignment 13.9. Write modulations using the German sixth chord as the pivot chord. Write in four parts the chords given and continue the modulation to the appropriate key. These may also be started in any other major key or in a minor key, and the ultimate key may be either major or minor,

a) G major: I ♯iv^{7G} = V^7 - - - - -
b) B major: I I ^{7} = ♯iv^{7G} - - - - -
c) B♭ major: I V^7 = ♯iv^{7G} - - - - -

Assignment 13.10. Write original compositions in chorale style or instrumental style, making use of any modulations studied in this chapter.

Assignment 13.11. Continue work in projects II-V, as assigned. Use modulations described under "Direct Modulation," "Modulation by Change of Mode," and "Modulation by Sequence" as well as pivot chord modulations.

Ear Training

Exercise 13.1. Harmonic dictation. When listening to a remote modulation, follow directions given in Chapter 1 for listening to modulations to closely related keys. When the pivot chord is a diminished seventh chord, identify the chord in the original key according to the directions given on pages 183–184, after which the dual nature of the pivot chord can be determined.

Keyboard Harmony

Exercise 13.2. At the keyboard, improvise modulations listed in Assignments 13.6 and 13.7.

Exercise 13.3. Improvise modulations between any two keys, using any diminished seventh as a pivot.

Exercise 13.4. Improvise modulations by lowering the root, third, or fifth of the diminished seventh chord (premature resolution). Figure 13.30 demonstrates the three possibilities using the vii^{d7} in C major (or C minor). The chord following the diminished seventh is used in the figure as a V^7 in the new key, but could also function as a secondary dominant or, respelled, as a German sixth chord.

Fig. 13.30.

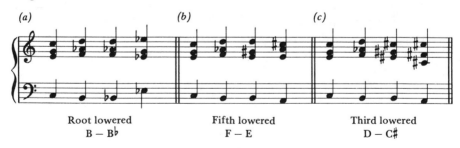

(a)	(b)	(c)
Root lowered	Fifth lowered	Third lowered
B – B♭	F – E	D – C♯

In addition to the above, these possibilities exist:

a) V^7-i in E♭ minor
      V^7-i in D♯ minor (V^7: B♭ D F A♭ = A♯ C$^\times$ E♯ G♯)

b) $V_{4\atop3}$-i in A minor

c) $V_{4\atop2}$I in F♯ major

$V_{4\atop2}$-I in G♭ major (V^7: C♯ E♯ G♯ B = D♭ F A♭ C♭)

Choose a key, then choose any diminished seventh chord in that key. Resolve the root, third, and fifth, in turn, down by half step, using the resulting chord as a V^7 in the new key.

Exercise 13.5.   Improvise modulations using the German sixth chord as one member of the pivot. Play each of the following in any key. Each may also be played when the original key is minor, when the new key is minor, or when both keys are minor.

a) I IV V I, I ♯iv^{7G} = V^7 I IV V I

b) I IV V I, I V^{7}ofIV = ♯iv^{7G} I$_6$ V I
    4

c) I IV V I, I V^7 = ♯iv^{7G} I$_6$ V I
    4

14

The End of an Era, and a Look Into the Twentieth Century

The compositional techniques of the historical period c.1650–c.1900 have been the subject of our study in this text and its preceding volume, *Elementary Harmony: Theory and Practice.* We have seen that no matter how each composer of this period differed from another in his particular style of writing, all were governed by certain concepts and practices, the body of which has come to be known as the common practice of the period. In review, the most important of these concepts and practices are:

1. *Tonality.* In every composition there is one tone which assumes more importance than the others, and to which the others are related. This phenomenon is emphasized by the almost exclusive use of V-I progression (authentic cadence) at the close of a composition and its liberal use elsewhere.

2. *Scale systems.* Tonality in this period is expressed through two scale systems, major and minor, other scale systems of earlier times having fallen into disuse (review *Elementary Harmony: Theory and Practice,* second edition, pp. 346–349).

3. *Keys.* Each major and minor scale can be found on fifteen different pitch locations, called keys. These keys are systematized in two circles of fifths, one for major and one for minor.

4. *Chords.* Music of the common practice period is based upon the use of chords. A chord is defined as a simultaneous sounding of pitches spelled, usually, in major and minor thirds, the lowest note of these thirds being considered the root. Not all possible chord constructions in thirds were regularly used.

5. *Inversion.* A chord retains its identity whether or not the root is found as the lowest sounding voice.

6. *Chord succession.* The progression of one chord to another is based upon the movement of their roots, root movement by fifth being the most common. Certain progressions tended to become much more widely used than others, and not all possible root relationships within a key were regularly used. Chord successions requiring the use of parallel fifths and/or octaves were carefully avoided.

7. *Non-harmonic tones.* Tones not belonging to a chord may sound simultaneously with a chord structure. Such a dissonance must always be introduced and resolved in certain established ways.

8. *Melody.* Melodic lines are so constructed that each tone will be part of a chord or an acceptable non-harmonic tone to that chord. A succession of melodic tones will usually imply an acceptable chord succession.

9. *Rhythm.* Rhythmic patterns are usually organized into metric units of two, three, and four beats, the primary accent falling on the first beat of any metrical group. Any other accent in any melodic line is a syncopation against the primary accent.

10. *Harmonic rhythm.* The rhythmic pattern created by the frequency of chord change conforms to the metric structures described in the preceding paragraph.

These, in most broad generalizations, are the basic concepts underlying the composition of music in the common practice period. Exceptions, though numerically quite frequent, actually represent only a very small percentage of the total output of the composers of the period. But this is not to imply that compositional techniques were stagnant and that no change in musical expression took place during this period of almost three hundred years. In any art form, in any science, in any institution, in life itself, change, for better or for worse, is the only constant known to human endeavor. The limitations listed above were subject to the attacks and inroads of change for the entire course of the historical period, so that by the end of the nineteenth century, no further change could take place within the style without destroying the style itself. True to predictable pressures of change, this is exactly what happened.

The sense of major and minor tonality bore the brunt of the forces of change, especially in the nineteenth century. The necessity for a chord progression to continue resolutely to its goal, the tonic, was often challenged, as we have seen, when resolution to the tonic was diverted or postponed temporarily by such devices as deceptive resolutions, progressions over a chromatic bass line, and successive diminished seventh chords, this latter being particularly effective in destroying temporarily any sense of key. More and more frequent use of chromatic tones blurred the impression of major and minor scales and decreased the importance of the tonic note, now one of twelve notes competing for importance rather than one of seven of the diatonic scale. Dissonances, which were originally of short duration and primarily for decorative purposes, become longer in duration, often almost as long as their accompanying chords, and more and more often were found in groups of two or three at a time. A frequent effect of these uses of dissonance was to produce the temporary impression of new chord structures not built in thirds.

All these and other endeavors to delay, weaken, and even subvert the function of the tonic culminated in the works of the middle and late nineteenth century, particularly in those of Richard Wagner. Any one sitting through the several hours' performance of *Tristan und Isolde* is constantly frustrated (or delighted, as the case may be) by the effects of dissonance and chromaticism in weakening tonality, especially by the lack of expected chord resolutions and by the varieties and frequencies of deceptive progressions to avoid positive establishment of a tonic. The late nineteenth-century style, as a result of the impact of this kind of writing, literally had no place to go. For a composer at this time to express original ideas in music, the only path led to more or less violent change through repudiation of any or all of the ten points listed at the beginning of this chapter. So the change came, a change as radical as that at the beginning of the seventeenth century[1] (review *Elementary Harmony: Theory and Practice*, pp. 341–346). What is more, this period of change is still with us. Composers of this century have been and still are constantly experimenting with new ideas and new techniques for expressing musical ideas. Consequently, it is impossible as yet to determine any "common practice" in the music of the twentieth century. Whether or not a common practice will ever emerge is an unanswered question, and even seems unlikely at this time, though we should remember, as a precedent, that Rameau's explanation of the basic concepts of the common practice period were formulated approximately 130 years after the advent of the new music of his time.

Without a basis of common practice, and until such is available, successful study and analysis of twentieth-century music is dependent upon systematic comparison of the new music with that of the period immediately preceding. The efforts of those first composers of "modern music" were directed to writing music which specifically would not sound like music of the common practice period; the music would therefore use compositional techniques and devices

---

[1] It must be understood that no specific date ever marks the change from one compositional period to another. In the earliest music to break away from the nineteenth-century style, there can be seen many features of the earlier period, as indeed can be seen in much music written up to the present day, especially in popular music, show music, and music written for pedagogical purposes. Many important composers of serious music, including such names as Sibelius, Mahler, Richard Strauss, and Rachmaninoff, continued writing well into the twentieth century, usually in a style best described as basically that of the common practice period. Their music consequently is often identified by the term "post-romantic."

not typical of and not represented in the writings of the common practice period.

It shall be the function of the remainder of this chapter to present some of the more significant of these new compositional techniques and devices. As a postscript to the study of traditional harmony, this chapter can make no pretense of being complete. Textbooks designed for the presentation and explanation of twentieth-century music must be consulted for this purpose.[2] Our purpose in this chapter is to demonstrate the relationship of current compositional practices to those of earlier periods, differentiating between those derived from earlier practices and those devised specifically to contradict earlier practices.

The best known of the earliest composers to make a definite break with the techniques of the common practice period was the French composer, Claude Debussy (1862–1918). A complete catalogue of the unique compositional practices introduced or made widely known through his genius would be excessively long for such a chapter as this. But some idea of his contributions to new compositional techniques can be observed in the following excerpts.

Debussy made extensive use of scales other than major and minor, both for use in melodic lines and as a basis for chord construction. One, the *whole tone scale*, equally divides the octave into six whole steps (Figure 14.1).

Fig. 14.1.

It is found in thirds in the upper clef of Figure 14.2, used contrapuntally against a single whole tone melodic line in the lower clef.

Fig. 14.2.

Debussy, *Préludes*, Book I, "Voiles"

---

[2] See Bibliography at the end of this chapter.

Only two chords built in thirds can be derived from this scale, C E G♯ and D F♯ A♯. These are used in Figure 14.3 to accompany the melodic line first seen in Figure 14.2.

Fig. 14.3.   Debussy, *Préludes*, Book I, "Voiles"

One transposition only of this scale is available: C♭ D♭ E♭ F G A. In Figure 14.4, chords derived from this scale but not built in thirds are found as the double dotted eighth notes: D♭ E♭ A and C♭ D♭ G. The missing note, F, is prominently stated in the vocal line. The chords found as thirty-second notes preceding each whole tone chord are made up of notes "non-harmonic" to the whole tone scale.

Fig. 14.4.   Debussy, *Trois Ballades de François Villon,*
                                        "Ballade de Villon à s'ayme"

Less frequently used is the *pentatonic scale,* found on the keyboard as the five black keys (Figure 14.5*a*) with several other possible transpositions. As before, this scale is used melodically and as a basis for chord construction.

Fig. 14.5.

(a)

Debussy, *Préludes*, Book I, "Voiles"

(b)

The resources of these two scales are relatively limited, and although they were effective in breaking away from the principles of common practice, their use is not characteristic of most other twentieth-century composers. The basic principle behind another scale, however, has served well throughout the century. This, the *contrived scale,* is simply a pattern made up of intervals of the composer's choosing. One such seen in Debussy is spelled A B C♯ D♯ E F G, like a major scale with ♯4 and ♭7.

Fig. 14.6.   Debussy, *L'Isle Joyeuse*

Parallelism, not to be countenanced in earlier periods, is a characteristic feature of the music of Debussy. Almost any chord combination can be found in parallel motion in his works. Parallel augmented triads were seen in Figure 14.3. Examples of other parallelisms involve major triads in Figure 14.7 and seventh chords in Figure 14.8.

Fig. 14.7.   Debussy, *Préludes,* Book I, "Le sons et les
                                                  parfums tournent dans l'air du soir"

©*Copyright 1910, Durand et Cie. Used by permission of the publisher. Elkan-Vogel, Inc., sole representative in the U.S.A.*

Fig. 14.8.   Debussy, *Pour le Piano,* "Sarabande"

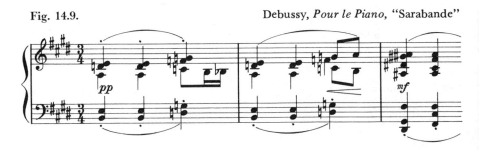

Up to the time of Debussy, chords built in thirds were the only ones possible. Of the many new possibilities for chord construction using other intervals, two are shown here. In Figure 14.9, chords built in fourths, B E A D and D G C F are found successively in measures 1–2 and A♯ D♯ G♯ with an added F♯ in measure 3. The chords of Figure 14.10 look like inversions of seventh chords, therefore built in thirds. But lacking the function of seventh chords, these are considered *chords of the added sixth,* for example, A C♯ E + F♯, G♯ B D♯ + E, etc., and are here found in parallel motion.

Fig. 14.9.   Debussy, *Pour le Piano,* "Sarabande"

Fig. 14.10.   Debussy, *Pour le Piano*, "Sarabande"

Having seen a few typical examples from Debussy, but by no means a comprehensive view of his innovations, we will look ahead to other composers and their compositional techniques in a more orderly fashion.

The compositional devices of the twentieth century can be roughly divided into two classifications, (1) those derived from the past, either as a revival after a long period of non-usage or those from the recent past used in new ways, and (2) those based upon new and original ideas unique to the twentieth century. Of the examples from Debussy, the whole tone scale had so little precedent in earlier music that it may be considered a new technique. The devices shown in the remaining examples all had roots in the past: the pentatonic scale (Figure 14.5) is common in ancient and contemporary Oriental cultures, among others; parallelism (Figures 14.7, 14.8) has its precedent in Medieval organum (review *Elementary Harmony: Theory and Practice,* Appendix 3); the contrived scale (Figure 14.6) is based upon the manipulation of a scale pattern already in exixtence; and construction of new chords (Figures 14.9, 14.10) continues the tradition of building vertical sonorities, but now based on intervals other than the third. We will continue first with compositional techniques based on earlier practices.

Melodic Resources

The Medieval modes, Dorian, Phrygian, Lydian, Mixolydian, and Aeolian (review *Elementary Harmony: Theory and Practice,* p. 347), have been revived and utilized by many twentieth-century composers after about three hundred years of non-use. Compositions are not, however, ordinarily written entirely in a given mode; rather, the mode adds a new scalar color during the course of the composition. One work based largely on a given mode, the Phrygian, is the *Fantasy on a Theme by Thomas Tallis,* written by Ralph Vaughan Williams. The theme is the Phrygian melody of a hymn by Tallis; it can be seen in *Music for Sight Singing* as number 543. A viola solo from this work begins in the Phrygian, changing in measure 5 to the Dorian on A and ending with a Picardy third of that mode.

Fig. 14.11.

Vaughan Williams, *Fantasy on a Theme by Thomas Tallis*

Other shorter uses of modal scales are most common during the present century. Another Phrygian melody, beginning and ending on the fifth of the scale, is seen in Figure 14.12.

Fig. 14.12.

Ravel, *Shéhérazade*, "La Flûte enchantée"

A long phrase in the Lydian mode on F in Figure 14.13 arrives at its cadence with the characteristic B♮ changed to B♭, giving an abrupt feeling of change to the major mode.

Fig. 14.13.

Sibelius, Symphony No. 4

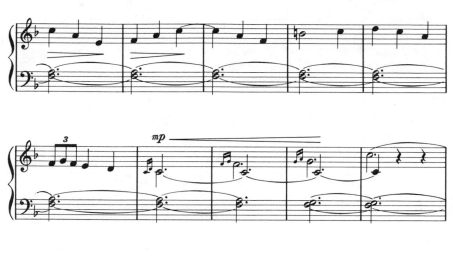

No longer tied to restrictions of the major and minor scales and the system of harmonic progression of previous centuries, twentieth-century composers found themselves free to write melodies that expressed no particular scale or harmonic patterns except those of the composer's choosing or construction. The first measure of Figure 14.14 uses each of the twelve notes of the chromatic scale,[3] and at the same time outlines the triads of G minor, E♭ minor, and two consecutive fourths.

Fig. 14.14.   Hindemith, Symphonie, *Mathis der Maler*

By permission of the publishers, B. Schott's Söhne, Mainz.

---

[3]This twelve-tone series is not used as a "tone row" or in the "twelve-tone technique" of Schoenberg, discussed later in this chapter.

Melodic lines, not being dependent upon an implied harmony, often sound independently of the harmony written against them; the tones of the melody in the bass clef of Figure 14.15 are neither part of the harmony nor non-harmonic to the chord progression above.

Fig. 14.15.   Schoenberg, *In diesen Wintertagen,* Op. 14, No. 2

Used by permission of Belmont Music Publishers, Los Angeles, California 90049.

The traditional concept of melody as a flowing stream of pitches was most radically challenged by a technique known as *pointillism,*[4] in which individual pitches are separated by wide leaps, usually dissonant, and punctuated by many rests. It can be argued, of course, whether or not the result of this kind of writing is, by definition, melodic. Nonetheless, this technique, devised by Webern, has had significant impact on many leading twentieth-century composers.

Fig. 14.16.   Webern, *Variationen für Klavier* (1936)

© *Copyright 1937 Universal Edition, Vienna. Used by permission of the publisher. Theodore Presser Company sole representative in the United States, Canada and Mexico.*

Chord Structures

In the examples from Debussy, we have seen several varying uses of chord structures, including both traditional chords used in non-traditional ways and

---

[4] Named after a technique of painting devised by Georges Seurat (1859–1891) in which the picture is made up of tiny dots or brush strokes.

chord structures not found in music of previous times. We may continue this phase of our study in the same manner.

Traditional chords, that is, chords built in thirds, are very common in the new styles, sometimes used exclusively in a composition and other times mixed with other types of chords. They are now free from the necessity of progressing by the favorite root movements of the preceding era, as in Figure 14.17, where a traditional analysis would reveal only a confusion of roman numeral symbols.

Fig. 14.17.   Fauré, *La Bonne Chanson*, Op. 61, "J'allais par des chemins perfides"

Modal melodies are often harmonized with chords of traditional construction, but in root progressions required by the modal scale pattern. The Mixolydian melody of Figure 14.18 uses triads built on ♭VII and v. In harmonizing the lowered seventh scale degree, a ♭III, containing a note not in the Mixolydian scale, is used. Note also the free use of parallel triads broken by the interpolation in two places of a single seventh chord and a pair of parallel seventh chords.

Fig. 14.18.   Vaughan Williams, *The Water Mill*

Chord structures in the twentieth century are free from classification as consonant or dissonant. A seventh chord, for example, may move freely as in Figure 14.18 without regard to preparation and resolution of the "dissonance." Differentiation of the quality of a chord structure is comparative: a given structure is either more dissonant or more consonant than another, but is neither dissonant nor consonant in itself.[5]

New chord structures seen in the Debussy examples were chords built in fourths and chords of the added sixth (Figures 14.9 and 14.10). In twentieth-century music, virtually no combination of notes to make up a harmonic sonority has been overlooked, ranging from the simple superimposition of fifths in Figure 14.19, to complex combinations of mixed intervals as in Figure 14.20.

Fig. 14.19.

Stravinsky, *Le Sacre du Printemps*

Fig. 14.20. Webern, *Fünf Lieder nach Gedichten von Stefan George,* Op. 4, "Ihr tratet zu dem Herde"

Seht was mit Trost - ge - ber - de der Mond euch rät: tre - tet

---

[5]A theory for establishing the relative consonance or dissonance of a chord structure was worked out by Paul Hindemith in his *Craft of Musical Composition*, New York, 1941.

weg vom Her - de, es ist wor - den spät,

An additional harmonic sonority, called a *cluster,* consists of three or more consecutive tones sounding simultaneously. Figure 14.21 shows alternating three-note clusters, A B C♯ and B♭ C D, used as a harmonic device. The six-note clusters of Figure 14.22 function as percussive accents in dramatizing the text.

Fig. 14.21.   Bartók, Quartet No. 4

Fig. 14.22. **Ives, from *Lincoln, the Great Commoner***

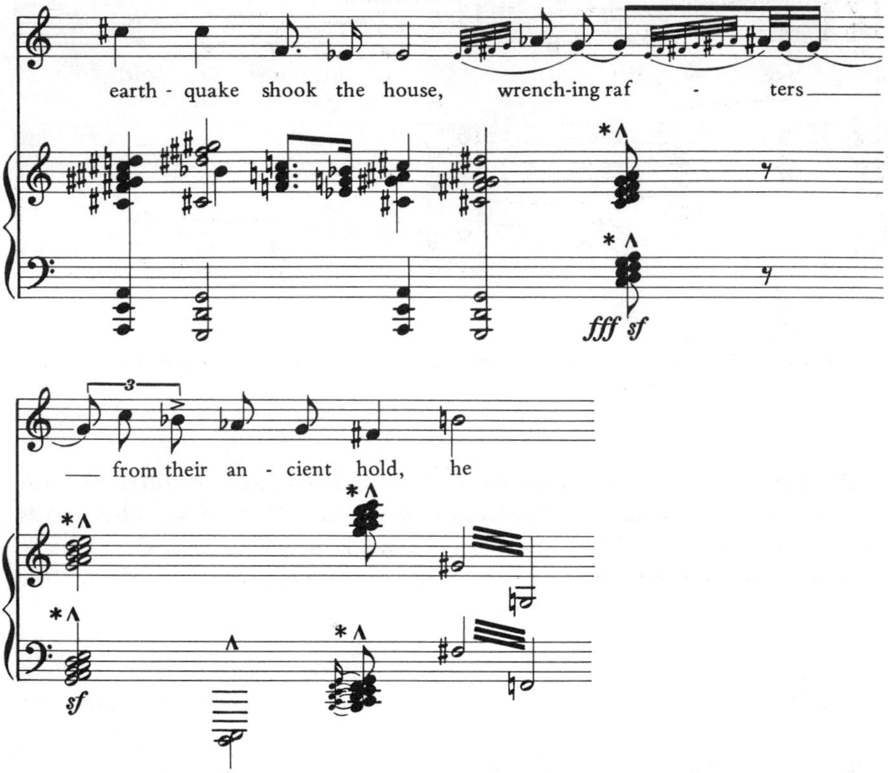

earth - quake shook the house, wrench-ing raf - ters
from their an - cient hold, he
fff sf
sf

*with the fist

Polytonality

Polytonality is the simultaneous sounding of more than one key, in practical usage, usually two. The forerunner of this device, the *polychord,* consisting of two distinct chord structures sounding simultaneously, is seen as early as Stravinsky's *Petrouchka,* the illustration from which shows the simultaneous sounding of C E G and F♯ A♯ C♯. See also Figure 14.30.

Fig. 14.23. Stravinsky, *Petrouchka*

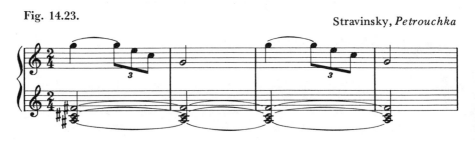

Polytonality requires that each of the two tonalities be unmistakably clear by itself. A simple example, Figure 14.24, shows a melodic line in one key, F Lydian, and its accompaniment in another, D♭ major.

Fig. 14.24.   Milhaud, *Trois Poémes de Jean Cocteau*, "Fête de Bordeaux"

Atonality

Although all the preceding examples display techniques not to be found in the period of common practice, all, with the exception of Figure 14.20, have one feature in common with that of the previous era. This is a sense of tonality, not necessarily described as major, minor, or even modal, but at least having a tone around which others gravitate (or two such tones in polytonality). But as early as the first decade of the twentieth century, a few composers attempted to break this strong link with the past by writing in such a way that a sense of traditional tonality was impossible or at least difficult to perceive. The principal composers working in this area were Arnold Schoenberg, Alban Berg, and Anton Webern: an example of atonal writing by the latter can be seen in Figure 14.20. As a result of experimentation in atonal writing, Schoenberg developed a system, described in his own words as a "Method of Composing with Twelve Tones Which are Related Only One with Another," but more popularly known as the "twelve-tone technique." As its goal, this technique makes it impossible for any one tone of the twelve to assume more importance than any other; therefore no single tone can assume the role of key center. These are the basic principles of this technique, and all are illustrated from Schoenberg's Fourth String Quartet:

1. The twelve tones of the octave are arranged in an order of the composer's choice. In this order they are known as the *tone row,* and this row is used as the basis for the composition.

Fig. 14.25.   Tone row for Schoenberg, Quartet No. 4

2. In the composition, no note of the row may be repeated, except for immediate repetitions, until all other eleven notes have been sounded.

Fig. 14.26.   Schoenberg, Quartet No. 4

3. The row may be transposed to begin on any other pitch. Octave transpositions of any note or notes are permissible. Observe also that the composer is free to cast any appearance of the row in any variety of rhythmic structure.

Fig. 14.27.   Schoenberg, Quartet No. 4

4. The row may be used harmonically as well as melodically. The first violin part of Figure 14.28 is the first two measures of Figure 14.26.

Fig. 14.28.   Schoenberg, Quartet No. 4

	1		2		3		4	5	6
Vln. 1	1		2		3		4	5	6
Vln. 2		4	9	11		7		12	2
Vla.		6	7	10		8		11	3
Cello		5	8	12		9		10	1

5. The row may be varied in these ways: *a) Inversion:* each melodic interval is the same size but proceeds in a direction opposite to that in the row, Figure 14.29*a*; *b) Retrograde:* the row begins with the twelfth note and progresses backwards through the row, Figure 14.29*b*; *c) Retrograde Inversion:* the row begins with the twelfth note and progresses to the first, but each interval is inverted in relation to the original row, Figure 14.29*c*. In all of these, transpositions of the entire row and octave transpositions of individual notes are admissible, as before.

Fig. 14.29.

(*a*) Inversion

Schoenberg, Quartet, No. 4

(*b*) Retrograde

(*c*) Retrograde Inversion

Copyright 1940 by G. Schirmer, Inc. Used by permission.

With four versions of the row, each transposable to twelve pitch locations, for a total of 48 combinations, and with freedom of octave transposition and rhythmic structure, the possibilities for composition in this technique are virtually limitless. Lacking in tonality in the traditional sense, the row itself becomes the tonality of the composition. Many refinements and variations on these basic techniques are found in the music of composers writing in this style, just as exceptional practices were found in music of earlier periods. This system as a whole has had an enormous influence on almost all the major composers since its inception in the early 1920s.[6]

---

[6]Music written in the twelve-tone technique is also known as *dodecaphony,* or *dodecaphonic* writing. The term *serialism* refers not only to this methodical arranging of pitches, but also to other factors such as duration of both sound and silence, dynamics, and timbre.

Meter and Rhythm

Meter and rhythm as used in earlier centuries still play an important role in twentieth-century music. The regularly recurring accents and measure lengths so typical of the common practice period are still found in much of the music written since 1900, as shown in some of the previous examples such as Figures 14.15, 14.18, 14.24, and 14.26. Of the three principal elements of music—melody, harmony, and rhythm—characteristics of nineteenth-century rhythm have been retained in the twentieth century to a much greater extent than those of melody or harmony.

A marked increase in the use of syncopation often gives the impression of a radical change in rhythmic practices. But if we define syncopation as the accenting of beats or parts of beats other than those of the regularly recurring accent, these being heard against a regular metric pattern, either sounded or implied, then at least in principle there is no change in style brought about by syncopation, except in degree. Increase in frequency was accompanied by more irregularity in the placement of syncopated notes in order to create rhythmic patterns not typical of the nineteenth century. The well-known example from Stravinsky, Figure 14.30, demonstrates an early and still exciting instance. The accents, however, being heard against an implied regular duple simple meter, still constitute syncopation in the accepted nineteenth-century meaning of the term.

Fig. 14.30.

Stravinsky, *Le Sacre du Printemps*

The success of jazz in the popular music field, with its emphasis on syncopation ranging from blatant and obvious to complex and subtle, has made its impact on some but not all composers of serious music. The "jazz" of Figure 14.31 includes *polyrhythm,* if we consider that the accents of the upper staff produce a $\frac{3}{8}$ meter sounding against the meter of the bass clef, which in this case is either the $\frac{4}{4}$ of the time signature or a $\frac{3}{4}$ beginning on each C♯.

Fig. 14.31.

Milhaud, *La Création du Monde* (1923)

By permission of Max Eschig, owner of copyright.

More significantly, twentieth-century composers have often returned to principles of rhythmic and metric structure commonly found in sixteenth-century musical composition. The rhythm of the music of that era, particularly vocal music, often seems extremely free and even unregulated by standards of the common practice period. Figure 14.32a is the first part of a song by John Dowland, quoted in full in *Music for Sight Singing,* number 544.[7] For our present figure, we have omitted bar lines, just as it was written in the sixteenth century. To ascertain the location of the accents, it becomes necessary to locate the accents in the poem. Then, by adding bar lines and time signatures as needed, we find we have a composition of changing meters. The four notes after the first quarter rest, for example, prove to be in $\frac{6}{8}$ meter in modern notation rather than syncopation in $\frac{3}{4}$ meter (Figure 14.32b).

Fig. 14.32.

Dowland, *Can She Excuse My Wrongs* (1597)

(a)

Can she ex - cuse my wrongs with vir-tue's cloak?   Shall I call her good

when she proves un - kind?

---

[7] In *Music for Sight Singing,* see also numbers 538, 540, 543.

(b)

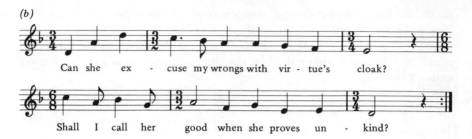

Can she ex - cuse my wrongs with vir - tue's cloak?

Shall I call her good when she proves un - kind?

Twentieth-century music makes extensive use of this irregular metric structure and is notated usually in one of two ways: (1) with a single time signature and regular barring, with the actual metrical accents to be determined by the performer as in Figure 14.33, or (2) by writing in each new time signature, especially in instrumental music where no poetic text is available.

Fig. 14.33.   Britten, *Five Flower Songs,* "To Daffodils"
Op. 47, No. 1

Fig. 14.34.

Copland, *Appalachian Spring*

Music in asymetric groupings such as 5, 7, or 11 and requiring time signatures such as $\frac{5}{4}$, $\frac{7}{8}$, $\frac{11}{4}$, or more complex, as $^{2+3+3}_8$, etc., are common in present-day music, but are by no means original in the twentieth century, as can be seen by examining the melodies, both folk and composed, in Chapter 19 of *Music for Sight Singing*.

New Sound Sources

In all the preceding examples, we have studied those factors which differentiated twentieth-century writing from that of earlier eras. Yet, no matter to what degree they have differed, there is still a remaining constant characteristic in common. In any era the sources of musical sound have been the same: the vibrating string, the vibrating air column, and the vibrating membrane. Therefore, the kind of sound for which composers write has been basically the same (though of course with constant refinements and improvements) from the time when man first blew on a reed, plucked a taut string, or struck a stretched skin.

The twentieth century has provided, for the first time in music history, new resources in sound itself. There are two varieties of such sounds: (1) electronic manipulation of natural sound and (2) electronic production of new sounds.

The first development in this area, known as *musique concrète*, combines old sound sources, including various forms of noise, with manipulation of these sounds by various techniques through the use of the tape recorder. A conventional sound or group of sounds is recorded on tape. The taped sounds can be manipulated in many ways, for example, by changing the speed of the machine or by reversing the tape. Tapes can be cut up and spliced together to achieve desired effects, and sounds from other sources can be superimposed upon existing taped sounds. These procedures, among others, provide a composer with almost unlimited possibilities for imaginative musical creation. There is no score for such a composition; the final tape is the score itself. No notation is required since the composition will be heard only when the tape is played on a machine. The effect of this kind of music is enhanced by stereo reproduction of the sounds on the tape using two and often more than two speakers.

Electronic music takes advantage of the fact that a vacuum tube or a transistor is capable of producing audible sound. These sounds can be organized and controlled, as in the electric organ, to the point where they can duplicate fairly realistically existing natural sounds such as those produced by orchestra and band instruments. But they can also produce a wide range of sounds never before heard by the ears of man. These sounds are produced on a machine known as a synthesizer,[8] which, to the uninitiated, recalls the complexities of a telephone switchboard or the dashboard of a Boeing 747. The synthesizer not only produces tones but can modify them in an almost unlimited number of ways. In addition to a wide variety of timbres, it is able to produce microtonal pitches, resulting in the possibility of creating scale formations with almost any number of desired equal tones to the octave. These sounds, along with *white noise,* a mixture of many simultaneous frequencies, are combined and juxtaposed in countless combinations on magnetic tape. Other sounds from nature, as in *musique concrète,* are often included as part of the texture of the completed composition.

Electronic music is performed in several ways: (1) by a playing of the completed tape alone, (2) by playing the tape along with an instrument or voice, or with an ensemble, with a conventional score for the conventional performers, and (3) by using the synthesizer as one of the instruments of the ensemble, played by a soloist with or without simultaneous performance of prerecorded tapes.

Computer music takes electronic music a step further. Here, the machine is the composer. The human element is the programmer who prepares for the computer a codification of the "styles" or "rules" within which the computer will do its work. The machine then produces random sounds within the programmed framework and these sounds are recorded on tape. According to the information fed to the computer, it can compose "original" music

---

[8]One commercial synthesizer, the Moog, has recently achieved popular notice through recordings on which the music of Bach and others is performed. Performance, though, is only a secondary function of this instrument.

varying in style from simple "pop" tunes to the most complex display of electronic sound combinations. Computer music may be considered "chance music" as described immediately below.

Chance Music

Chance music, also called *aleatory music* or *music of indeterminancy,* is a natural reaction to the highly organized techniques of serialism. The earliest form of chance music is the "jamming" by a jazz combo, free improvisation by several instruments simultaneously based on a given tune and chord progression.[9] Music written as chance music, however, gives the performer and sometimes the conductor the choice of what to play, when, and for how long from a group of composed possibilities, or improvisation on any of these possibilities or any combination of score reading and improvisation. Conventional instruments, electronic instruments, prerecorded tapes, and human voices may join in the chance or improvisatory ensemble. Works in conventional style (to be played as written) often include sections in aleatory style.

New Notation

Conventional notation, with its emphasis on exact delineation of duration and pitch within the tempered system of tuning, will not serve to specify sounds emanating from a synthesizer or to describe the procedures for the performance of chance music. Consequently, new forms of notation are being developed. At present there is little standardization of these notational practices, since each composer develops a system to express that which he is trying to achieve.

Figure 14.35 shows an example of just such notation. The work from which this is an excerpt is written for a conventional symphony orchestra using a conventional orchestral score. One section of the work, however, is aleatory, making use of both conventional instruments and electronic sounds. Our figure shows the score for the electronic sounds in this aleatory section; additional pages in this section provide aleatory passages for each of the string, woodwind, brass, and percussion sections of the orchestra. From these pages, the conductor during the performance chooses, and indicates by hand signals (two of which are shown), which "events" will be played by the respective sections of the orchestra. He is free to select in any order any passage or any combination of passages, and to continue the aleatory part of the piece for as short or as long a time as he pleases. Successive performances of this work, then, will usually differ greatly from each other.

---

[9] Realizing a figured bass in eighteenth-century instrumental style contains, of course, restricted elements of chance.

Fig. 14.35. Merrill Ellis, *Kaleidoscope*

The circle at the top of the page represents a prerecorded endless tape loop containing several "events" as pictured around the circle. At the given hand signal, the tape is played, beginning at random at any point on the circle, or, a live performer at the keyboard of a synthesizer may choose any point on the circle and improvise according to the diagram at that point. Among the many notational devices shown, we will describe a few: (1) the horn-like symbol at the left represents crescendo of a tone, rise in pitch, addition of pitches to be sounded simultaneously, and a modulating timbre, indicated, reading left to right, as a change from a "sine" wave to a "square" wave; (2) white noise sounds at the upper right are indicated in only approximate pitch locations; (3) conventional notation at the botton of the circle is combined with electronic instructions. A different hand signal will cue in one of the prerecorded ostinato patterns at the bottom of the score.

Other scores for aleatory and electronic compositions by other composers may or may not contain notational symbols found in this excerpt, and all will contain many symbols not found here. Successful performance of such a composition as this depends upon the clarity of the composer's instructions and notational devices and upon the understanding by the conductor of the principles and methods of electronic composition.

Summary

Music of the last half of the twentieth century finds composers heading in many directions, using exclusively or in any combination the tone row, serialism, systematic or non-systematic principles of harmonic and contrapuntal development, electronics, and indeterminacy. As the century proceeds, expansion of experimentation seems to be the order of the day rather than consolidation of the achievements of earlier decades. Consequently, the present volatile state of the art may continue for some time before the true accomplishments of the century are known and a rational and comprehensive theory of the music can be developed. For the student and listener, this means that an understanding of new developments as they occur depends in great part upon the ability to analyze new sounds and techniques and to compare them with known practices both of the recent past and of previous eras.

BIBLIOGRAPHY

Austin, William W., *Music in the 20th Century*. New York: W. W. Norton & Company, Inc., 1966.

Cope, David H., *New Directions in Music—1950–1970*. Dubuque, Iowa: Wm. C. Brown Company, Publishers, 1971.

Dallin, Leon, *Techniques of Twentieth Century Composition* (2nd ed.). Dubuque, Iowa: Wm. C. Brown Company, Publishers, 1964.

Hansen, Peter, *An Introduction to Twentieth Century Music* (2nd ed.). Boston: Allyn and Bacon, Inc., 1967.

Machlis, Joseph, *Introduction to Contemporary Music.* New York: W. W. Norton & Company, Inc., 1964.

Marquis, G. Welton, *Twentieth Century Music Idioms.* Englewood Cliffs, N.J.: Prentice-Hall, Inc., 1964.

Persichetti, Vincent, *Twentieth-Century Harmony.* New York: W. W. Norton & Company, Inc., 1961.

Salzman, Eric, *Twentieth Century Music: An Introduction.* Englewood Cliffs, N.J.: Prentice-Hall, Inc., 1967.

Stuckenschmidt, H. H., *Twentieth Century Music.* New York: McGraw-Hill Book Company, 1969.

Ulehla, Ludmila, *Contemporary Harmony.* New York: The Macmillan Company, 1966.

Appendix 1

The Essentials of Part-Writing

THE SINGLE CHORD

Approximate Range of the Four Voices

Soprano: d^1-g^2 Alto: a-c^2
Tenor: f-f^1 Bass: F-c^1

Triad Position

In *open position*, the distance between the soprano and tenor is an octave or more. In *close position*, the distance between the soprano and tenor is less than an octave. The distance between adjacent voices normally does not exceed an octave, although more than an octave may appear between bass and tenor.

Normal Doubling

Diatonic major and minor triads
  a) root in bass: double the root
  b) first inversion: double the soprano note
  c) second inversion: double the bass note
  d) exception, minor triads, root or third in bass: the third of a minor triad is often doubled, particularly when this third is the tonic, subdominant, or dominant note of the key.
  Diminished triad (usually found in first inversion only): double the third; when the fifth is in the soprano, the fifth is usually doubled.
  Augmented triad: double the bass note.
  Seventh chord: normally, all four voices are present. In the major-minor seventh chord, the root is often doubled and the fifth omitted.
  Altered triad: normally, same doubling as non-altered triads; avoid doubling the altered note.

CHORD CONNECTION

Triad Roots

When the bass tones of two successive triads are the *roots* of the triads
Triad roots are repeated.
Rule 1.   Both triads may be written in the same position, or each may
be in different position. Triad positions should be changed
   a) when necessary to keep voices in correct pitch range
   b) when necessary to keep correct voice distribution (two roots, one third,
and one fifth).
   c) to avoid large leaps in an inner part
Triad roots are a fifth apart.
Rule 2A.   Retain the common tone; move the other voice stepwise.
Rule 2B.   Move the three upper voices in similar motion to the nearest
tones of the next triad.
Rule 2C.   Move the third of the first triad up or down the interval of a
fourth to the third of the second triad, hold the common tone and move
the other voice by step.
Rule 2D.   (Exception) At the cadence, the root of the final tonic triad may
be tripled, omitting the fifth.
Triad roots are a second apart.
Rule 3.   The three upper voices move contrary to the bass.
Triad roots are a third apart.
Rule 4A.   Hold the two common tones; the other voice moves stepwise.
Rule 4B.   When the soprano moves by leap, the second triad may be in
either close or open position.
Rule 5.   When it is impossible or undesirable to follow normal rules for
triads with roots in bass, double the third in the *second* of the two triads. But
if this third is the leading tone or any altered tone, double the third in the
first of the two triads.

Triads in Inversion

Progression to or from a triad in *inversion,* a triad with a *doubled third,* or
a triad with any *unusual doubling*
Rule 6A.   Write the two voices moving to or from the doubled note first,
using oblique or contrary motion if possible.
Rule 6B.   When first inversions of triads are found in succession, each triad
must have a different doubling to avoid parallel octaves, or the same doubling
may appear in different pairs of voices. Avoid doubling the leading tone or
any altered tone. Approach and leave each doubled tone using Rule 6A.

Position Changes

Rule 7.   Triad position may be changed
  a) at a repeated triad.
  b) using Rule 2C.
  c) at a triad in inversion or a triad with unusual doubling, following Rule 6A.

Non-Harmonic Tones

Rule 8.   A non-harmonic tone temporarily replaces a harmonic tone. Write the triad with normal doubling if possible and substitute the non-harmonic tone for one of the chord tones. Approach and leave the non-harmonic tone according to the definition of the non-harmonic tone being used.

Seventh Chords

Rule 9.   The seventh of a seventh chord, its note of approach, and its note of resolution comprise a three-note figure similar to certain non-harmonic tone figures: passing tone, suspension, appoggiatura and upper neighbor. The seventh usually resolves down by step.

Altered Chords

Rule 10.   Use of altered chords does not change part-writing procedure. Do not double altered note. Follow Rule 6A if unusual doubling occurs. A lowered altered tone usually proceeds downwards; a raised altered tone proceeds upwards. *Exception:* the altered root of a major triad may be doubled; one of these roots is usually resolved by leap.

General Rule

Rule 11.   In situations not covered by Rules 1–10, observe the following:
  a) Move each voice the shortest distance possible.
  b) Move the soprano and bass in contrary or oblique motion if possible.
  c) Avoid doubling the leading tone, any altered note, any non-harmonic tone, or the seventh of a seventh chord.
  d) Avoid parallel fifths, parallel octaves, and the melodic interval of the augmented second.

Appendix 2

Instrumentation:
Ranges, Clefs, Transposition

Range

The range given for each instrument is approximately that ordinarily used by the average player. Neither the lowest nor the highest note playable by the instrument is necessarily included. These ranges will be found satisfactory for purposes of this text.

Clef

Each instrument regularly uses the clef or clefs found in the musical illustrations under "Range." Exceptions or modifying statements are found under the heading "Clef."

Transposition

Unless otherwise indicated under this heading, pitches given under "Range" sound concert pitch when played. (Concert pitch: $A^1 = 440$ vibrations per second; the note A^1 on the piano keyboard is concert A). All transposing instruments sound their name when written C is played; for example, a Clarinet in B♭ sounds B♭ when it plays a written C.

STRING INSTRUMENTS

Violin

Viola

Clef. Alto clef is used almost exclusively. Treble clef is used occasionally for sustained high passages.

Violoncello (´Cello)

Clef. Bass clef is ordinarily used. Tenor clef is used for extended passages above small A. Treble clef is used for extreme upper range (not shown).

Double Bass (Bass Viol, Contrabass)

Transposition. Notes sound an octave lower than written.

WOODWIND INSTRUMENTS

Flute

Oboe

Clarinet: B♭ and A

Transposition.

a) Clarinet in B♭. Notes sound a major second lower than written. Use signature for the key a major second *above* concert pitch.

b) Clarinet in A. Notes sound a minor third lower than written. Use signature for the key a minor third *above* concert pitch.

Bassoon

Range

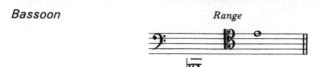

Clef.   Bass clef is ordinarily used. Tenor clef is used for upper range.

English Horn (Cor Anglais)

Range

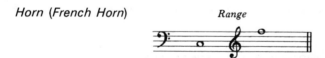

Transposition.   Notes sound a perfect fifth lower than written. Use signature for the key a perfect fifth *above* concert pitch.

Horn (French Horn)

Range

Clef.   Treble clef is commonly used.

Transposition.   Notes sound a perfect fifth lower than written. Key signatures are not ordinarily used. Write in all accidentals. In many published horn parts, notes written in the bass clef sound a perfect fourth higher than written. Consult with player of instrument before writing horn part in bass clef.

Horn parts are occasionally written in D, E♭, and E.

Saxophones: E♭ Alto, B♭ Tenor, and E♭ Baritone

Range

Transposition.

    a) E♭ Alto Saxophone. Notes sound a major sixth lower than written. Use signature for the key a major sixth *above* concert pitch.

    b) B♭ Tenor Saxophone. Notes sound a major ninth (an octave plus a major second) lower than written. Use signature for the key a major second *above* concert pitch.

    c) E♭ Baritone Saxophone. Notes sound an octave plus a major sixth lower than written. Use signature for the key a major sixth *above* concert pitch.

BRASS INSTRUMENTS

Trumpet or Cornet, B♭ and C

Transposition.

    a) Trumpet or Cornet in B♭. Notes sound a major second lower than written. Use signature for the key a major second *above* concert pitch.

    b) Trumpet or Cornet in C. Non-transposing—sounds as written.

Trombone

    Clef.   Both tenor and bass clefs are commonly used.

Tuba

Index